The Piccolo Craft Book

Also in Piccolo

Deborah Manley
The Piccolo All the Year Round Book

Deborah Manley and Pamela Cotterill
Maps and Map Games

Deborah Manley, Peta Ree and Margaret Murphy
The Piccolo Holiday Book

Deborah Manley and Peta Ree
Piccolo Picnic Book
Piccolo Book of Games for Journeys
Piccolo Book of Parties and Party Games

Deborah and Roy Manley
The Piccolo Book of Cartoons

Deborah Manley and Diane James

The Piccolo Craft Book

cover illustration by Carol Lawson text illustrations by Juliet Stanwell-Smith

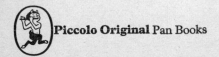 Piccolo Original Pan Books

First published 1977 by Pan Books Ltd,
Cavaye Place, London SW10 9PG
© Deborah Manley and Diane James 1977
ISBN 0 330 25188 0
Printed and bound in Great Britain by
Richard Clay (The Chaucer Press) Ltd, Bungay, Suffolk

Contents

Introduction

This book isn't going to make you into a skilled craftsman. Not overnight anyway. What we have tried to do is to introduce you to a large number of different crafts and to give you enough guidance so that you can actually make something. If you then find that you like the materials you have been working with, have enjoyed the skills you have been using and are satisfied with the results of your work, then you will want to go on in order to perfect your craftsmanship.

To do this, you may need to read further (there is a book list at the back of this book and there are many, many other books and pamphlets which will help you). You will certainly want to talk to other people who are interested in the same craft and discuss their methods and experiences. Often the craft suppliers (also listed at the end of the book) will be very willing to give helpful advice.

Once you have begun – carry on. Practice at a craft, as in most things, may not always make perfect, but it certainly leads towards perfection. But even more important, we think, is that working skilfully with your hands to create things gives enormous pleasure. It certainly has to us.

1 Using needle and thread

Making a sampler

An old proverb from Arabia says, 'Embroidery signifies a lack of work', but ever since earliest cavemen discovered they could join skins together by using a crude bone needle, people all over the world have been using needle and thread to decorate their clothes, furniture and sometimes even the walls of their homes. You can see many examples of old pieces of embroidery in books and museums. These range from the rich, exotic court dresses worked with golden threads on silk and velvet, to simple, coarse, brilliantly coloured peasant designs. Some large pieces were worked by a whole group of people and tell a story, like the Bayeux Tapestry which tells the story of William the Conqueror and the Battle of Hastings.

There are only a few basic embroidery stitches which you need to master before you can start experimenting and making up your own. You can use almost any kind of thread and material, but you would find it difficult to use a thick woollen thread on a fine silk!

Embroidery Stitches
Running stitch

This is the easiest stitch of all. You work from right to left taking the needle over and under the material and making the stitches an even length on both sides. When you have worked a row of running stitch you can weave a different coloured thread through the stitches. The brightly coloured borders you see on many Greek and Bulgarian clothes are made by using just simple running stitches of varying lengths and colours.

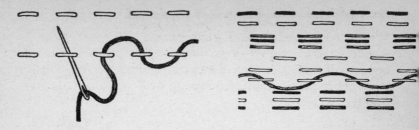

Back stitch

Bring your needle through to the right side of the material, make a small stitch backwards and then bring the needle through to the right side a little in front of the stitch you have just made, and then back again into the beginning of the first stitch.

Pekinese stitch

This stitch is made by weaving another colour of thread in a loop formation over a row of running stitch.

Chain stitch

Bring your needle through to the right side of the material. Leave a loop of thread on the surface of the material and pass the needle back through close to the first stitch. Bring the needle back up where you want the first link of the chain to end and through the loop you have made. Now start from the beginning again. Although chain stitch is usually used as an outline stitch you can also use it as a filling-in stitch.

Cross stitch

Work a row of stitches slanting either to the right or left. Now work back across them with the same size of stitch slanting in the opposite direction. You can make a double cross stitch by working a row of horizontal stitches followed by a row of vertical stitches over the original cross.

double cross stitch   satin stitch

Satin stitch

This is used as a filling stitch, but you shouldn't try to cover too large an area with one stitch. Work straight stitches side by side, as close together as possible across the area you want to fill.

Overstitch

This is a very simple way of finishing the edge of a fraying material. Bring the needle through about 1 cm from the edge.

Pass the thread over the edge of the material and bring the needle through again about 1 cm ($\frac{1}{2}$ in) along. Continue until you have completed the edge.

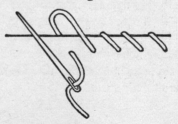

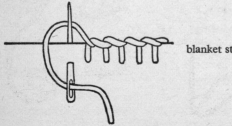

blanket stitch

Blanket stitch

Blanket stitch can be used either as a decorative stitch on embroidery or as an edging to a piece of cloth, as we use it in this book. If you are using a material that frays, turn it over at the edge. Bring the needle through a little in from the edge. Then take a downward stitch towards the edge of the material with the thread under the point of the needle. Tighten the stitch to lie along the edge of the cloth. You may find that you have blankets in your house that have this stitch at the top and bottom.

Now that we have explained the basic stitches, and you have tried them out on a scrap of material, you might like to make a 'sampler' to keep as a reference. Over four hundred years ago young girls were expected to make a sampler of the stitches they knew before they started on more advanced embroidery. If you want to make yours similar to those worked by your ancestors it should include your name, age, the alphabet, and a verse, such as this one which appeared on a sampler worked by a nine-year-old girl in the eighteenth century:

> Dear mother as I am young and cannot show
> Such work as I unto your goodness owe,
> Be pleased to smile on this my small endeavour.
> I'll strive to learn and be obedient ever.

Work out your design on a piece of paper first. Victorian samplers usually had deep borders, and the spaces between the verse, alphabet and name were filled with simple patterns and pictures of houses, dogs, trees, flowers and birds. It would be best to work on a fine canvas to begin with as the holes will help you to keep the stitches even, and will make the planning easier. Try to use all the stitches you know, and experiment with different colours. If you have an embroidery hoop or frame in which to hold your cloth you will find it easier to work extra neatly!

Assisi embroidery

Assisi is one of the most lovely of the many beautiful Italian hill towns. At one end of the town is the basilica of St Francis, the saint of birds and animals and lover of the poor, who lived in Assisi and founded the Franciscan order of monks.

The town is also famous for its embroidery, which has been taken by nuns to all parts of the world and taught to the children in their

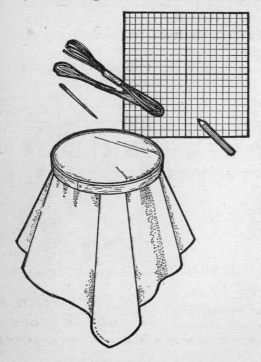

convents. Assisi embroidery traditionally uses blue or rust coloured thread to fill in the background, leaving the design or picture standing out in the creamy-white material. A running stitch in black or another dark colour is used to outline the design.

The materials you will need are:

Natural coloured cloth with an open weave (some needlework shops will have special Assisi cloth).
Stranded *embroidery cotton* in blue or rust and black or a dark colour
Embroidery hoop
Embroidery needle
Squared *graph paper* and a *pencil* with which to draw your design

Here are two simple traditional Assisi designs, which show the usual animals and birds beloved of St Francis, with a formal border. You can, when you get more skilful, make complete scenes in Assisi embroidery. We show also how one of these designs can be transferred on to your squared paper so that you have a pattern to follow. Although you may prefer, at least at the start, to buy a transfer pattern which you can iron on to your cloth.

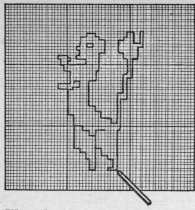

The embroidery stitches

Use one or two strands of embroidery cotton depending on the thickness of the material.

The outlines

You start by working the outlines using your dark thread and running stitch (see page 7), going first one way and then back over the work to make a continuous line. Work the first outline taking stitches across three threads of fabric on the top of the cloth, and bringing your needle up after three threads below.

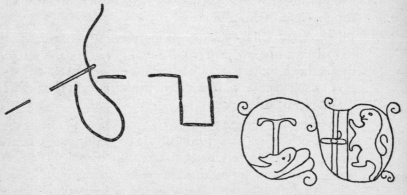

Continue like this round the object to be outlined. If there is any pattern or shaping within the design, work these at the same time in running stitch.

The background

Now you will work in cross stitch (see page 9). Work the up stroke of the crosses right across each part of the design, counting three threads of the material for each stitch. Then work back across the diagonals to make the cross. The back of your Assisi work should be as fine as the front.

The border

When you have finished the main design, work the outer border which will usually have an outline in cross stitch set slightly away (three threads) from the main background.

Patchwork

Patchwork and rag rug making (which is explained on pages 45–7) were both created originally from the necessity for poor people to use very scrap of cloth for as long as it lasted. Now patchwork has returned as a very popular craft, and there are many different ways to make it. Here we will show you only a few of them.

Patchwork made up of hexagonal or six-sided pieces

We suggest that you start with a cushion cover, which is a satisfying thing to make and not as difficult as the quilts which many people start and then never finish! It will help you to learn the principles of this craft.

First you must collect your scraps together. All your patches must be of the same type of material. For example, if you use cotton, all the patches must be cotton. You can use any piece you wish, but here we suggest that you use a combination of light patterned and darker plain cotton pieces.

If you are lucky enough to have a 'rag bag' or scrap drawer in your home you will find no difficulty in collecting your pieces. (Make sure you ask permission to take them though!) If not, then we suggest that, as for rag rugs, you search for materials at jumble sales. Ideally patchwork material should be new, but you can often pick up lengths of cloth or almost new cotton dresses at such sales.

Making your template

The template is the pattern from which all the pieces are cut. A few needlework shops sell metal templates, but you can make your own out of strong card.

1 With a compass draw a circle with a diameter (A–B) of 5 cm (2 in). Draw a line across the centre (C) with a ruler.

2 Using your compass again or with dividers, fix the points the same distance apart as the radius of the circle (A–C or B–C). Now put one point at A and mark points D and E. Move the compass point on to B and mark points F and G.

3 Now join the points D and G, and E and F with your ruler. You have now divided your circle into six equal parts.

4 With your ruler, join the points on the circumference round the circle.

5 Cut your six-sided template along these lines.

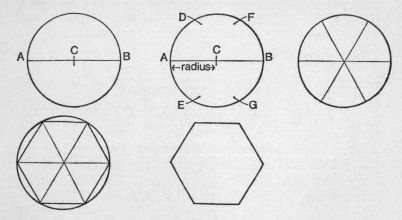

It is quite useful also to make a 'window' template which will help you to choose the piece to use out of a patterned material. Make another hexagon in the same way but about 2 cm (¾ in) larger in circumference. Cut a hexagonal window in it the same size as the original hexagon by tracing round the template. You can now hold this 'window' over the patterned material to select the best piece.

 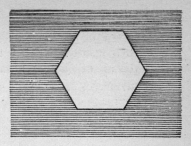

Cutting the patches

First you have to cut a great number of firm paper pieces using your template. You baste or tack all the cloth pieces on to these paper pieces in order to keep the work firm and flat while you sew it together.

Then cut your cloth pieces about 1 cm ($\frac{1}{2}$ in) larger all round than the template. Always place the template so one edge runs along the straight weave of the cloth. This will also help your patchwork to lie flat.

Preparing your pieces

Each piece of cloth now has to be tacked on to one of your backing papers. Place the patch on the centre of the paper. Turn the edges of the cloth down around the paper hexagon. Tack it on through all the layers. Keep the corners as flat as you can.

When you have enough pieces of the right colours prepared in this way, you can start to sew them together. For your cushion we suggest that you start with a light patterned piece at the centre with a darker plain row round it and a lighter row round that.

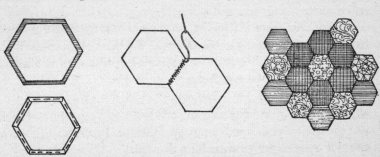

Sewing up your patches

Oversew the patches together from the back. Use simple and small oversewing stitches, through the edge of the material. Some of the stitches will go through the edge of the papers too. Not too many, or you may have trouble removing the papers. Leave all the papers in place until you have completed the whole work. This will help to keep it smooth.

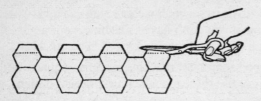

When your work is as big as you want it, you can square it off straight along the edges by cutting across the hexagons jutting out.

Completing your work

Most patchwork needs to be lined. Use a cotton lining for cotton patchwork; silk lining for silk or velvet patchwork. Your cushion cover will not need a lining, but we explain how to line patchwork for future reference. Lay your work out flat on the lining material. Turn in the edges of both the lining and the patchwork. Tack the two pieces of material together.

For a quilt you would then oversew the top to the backing cloth all round. For your cushion cover you need only oversew the back and the front together to form the side seams. Remember to leave one side open to put your cushion through!

Patchwork is delicate and the colours may run, so, when it needs cleaning, either wash it by hand in warm water with soap suds or have it dry-cleaned.

At the end of this section we show a number of things which you can make with your pieces of patchwork.

Machine patchwork

If you know how to use a sewing machine, you can make patchwork very quickly. Even if you don't have a machine, you can use this method, although the pieces won't go together so quickly.

There are two good shapes for machine patches – squares and rectangles. You can use these to make four different designs, like these:

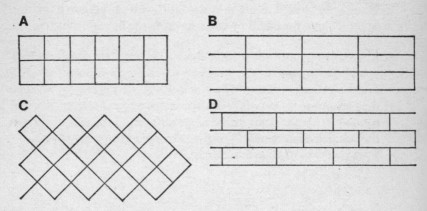

Decide on your colour scheme and on how large you want your patches to be. A 10-cm (4-in) square or an 8-cm (3-in) by 15-cm (6-in) rectangle are quite good size pieces to start with. Cut a good pile of pieces to the right size.

Using straight squares or rectangles (A and B)

Lay your pieces out so that you can decide how your pattern will go. Then collect the pieces from each row together in separate piles, in the order you want them to be. Sew each pile into a long strip using either your sewing machine or, if you are sewing by hand, using running stitch with an occasional back stitch.

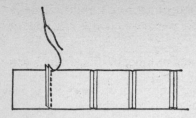

Make sure that you keep the seam on each piece the same width, about 1 cm ($\frac{3}{8}$ in). When your strips are completed press the seams open and flat.

Now sew your strips together, making sure that each piece is directly beneath the one above. Press the seams again. Your piece of patchwork is now complete and ready to be made up into the planned article.

Diagonal squares (C)

If you plan to use your squares diagonally (like 'square diamonds') you sew them together in the same way as we have described above, but the lengths of the strips will vary greatly according to whether they are at the corner of the work or across the middle, as you can see on picture C. To make the edges square, you simply cut across the squares from corner to corner, leaving a little extra on each square to turn in, to avoid fraying.

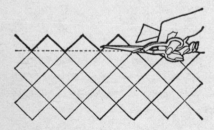

Brickwork (D)

For this sort of patchwork you work in exactly the same way while you are joining the pieces into strips. The difference comes when you are joining the strips together. The seams must be positioned at the centre of the patch above and below. To square off the edges you simply cut off the pieces of each rectangle that are jutting out.

Decorated patchwork

Using the basic methods described above you can create a new dimension by adding embroidery and appliquéd pieces to your patchwork.

Following the instructions for appliqué given on pages 30–31, sew the pieces on to the patches of the patchwork when you have joined them together. But do this before you back it or make it up into a cushion or whatever you plan to do. You can add such designs as flowers, letters, faces or abstract patterns. When one of us made patchwork quilts for her children, she used to embroider their names on to one piece (sometimes a larger piece than the others) before sewing the piece into the patchwork.

This has been only a simple introduction to patchwork. Once you have acquired the skill, there are an enormous variety of other patchwork designs you can try, using triangles, small shapes, mixed shapes and even circles. You can also use small pieces of patchwork for decoration on a plain background.

This picture shows some of the things which you might like to make from the different sorts of patchwork we have shown you. You can use the pattern for the crochet tabard on page 58 to make a patchwork tabard like the one shown here.

American Indian bead embroidery

There cannot be many people who have never made a string of beads! Neolithic man living over 10,000 years ago was no exception. His beads were seeds and berries strung on rough twine or stitched to animal skins with a bone needle. Remains of Egyptian beadwork have been found dating back to 4000 years BC, but beads were not always used for decoration. The word bead comes from the Anglo-Saxon word 'bede' meaning a prayer, and today strings of rosary beads are used for counting prayers. Beads were also used as an aid to counting, in the form of the abacus which is still used in some Eastern countries today in place of the modern cash register!

But perhaps the most important use of beads was as a means of exchange before people used money. The early colonists in America used beads to trade with the Indians, and these trading beads were known as 'wampum'. Different coloured beads signified different values and purple beads were worth twice as much as white ones. Apart from trading with beads the Indians were experts in the art of using beads to decorate their clothes, belts, shoes and moccasins. They used different methods of beading; one using a needle and thread, and the other a simple loom. Neither of these methods is complicated and after a little practice you will be able to make bracelets or arm-bands, necklaces, head-bands, bags and belts, like the American Indians made.

Threading beads

You will need a supply of different coloured beads, some strong thread and a long thin beading needle. If you want to follow the Indian style of beading use the smallest size beads, which are usually sold by the ounce in craft shops. It is best to sort the beads into separate colours and put them in shallow plastic containers. One of the easiest patterns to start with is the 'flower-head'. You can be making a necklace whilst you learn the technique! To make a necklace using the flower pattern you need two different colours of bead (we will call them black and white in the instructions). Thread your beading needle with a strong thread (transparent fishing twine would be ideal) and make a knot in the end. Using your needle, pick up five white beads and then one black bead, (this black bead will be the centre of the flower). Pass the needle UP through the first white bead, and pick up three more white beads. Pass the needle DOWN through the white bead immediately before the black one, and your flower is complete!

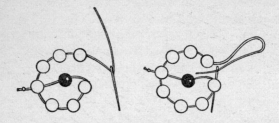

Now you start from the beginning again. Instead of starting with five white beads you could reverse the colours and use the white for the centre of the flower. Carry on threading until the necklace is the length you want. Join the first flower head to the last by threading your needle through both sets of beads several times, and hide the end by threading back through several beads. If you need to join your thread at any stage, make a firm knot with long ends which you can thread in afterwards.

Loom beading

Loom weaving gives a much more solid beading effect, as all the beads lie in straight lines. Bead looms are not expensive, but if you want to start weaving straight away you could make your own from an old shoe box. Cut small V-shaped nicks in the narrow ends of the box, about 5 mm ($\frac{1}{4}$ in) apart. The number of nicks depends on how wide your finished piece of beading is to be, the length of the box will determine the length of the beading.

Another method of making a loom is to hammer in nails (again 5 mm or $\frac{1}{4}$ in apart) at either end of a piece of wood of the length you want your beading to be.

In either case the next step is to attach the warp threads (these are the lengthwise threads). These threads must be strong, such as button thread or else rubbed with beeswax which will make the thread less likely to break. You need one more warp thread than the number of beads in one row of your pattern. If you are using the shoe box loom, slot the warp threads into the nicks and secure them under the box with sellotape. With the nail loom you can wind the warp threads round the nail heads and secure them with a firm knot. Your loom is now ready for weaving.

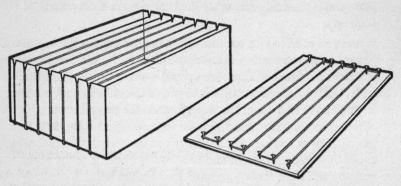

You can follow traditional Indian patterns or invent your own. The best way to make a pattern is to draw your design on graph paper. Allow one square for each bead, and colour the squares to show what the finished pattern will look like. To start weaving, thread your beading needle with a strong weft thread (the weft carries the beads across the warp). Attach the weft to the outside warp thread on the top left hand corner of the loom. Thread the correct number of beads on to the needle (one less than the number of warp threads). Slide the beads down to the knot, keeping them UNDER the warp threads. With your left hand push up one bead into each space between the warp threads (now you will see why

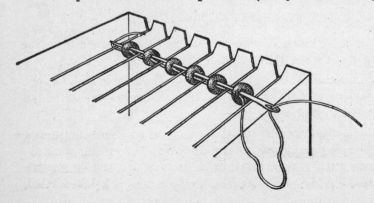

you needed the extra warp thread). Pass the needle back through the beads, on TOP of the warp threads. Thread the second row of beads in the same way, passing the beads UNDER first and the needle carrying the weft OVER the warp threads and through the beads. Once you have got used to the technique you can follow your graph pattern, picking up the beads in the right colour sequence.

When you need to join your thread make the knot in the middle of a row so that the beads will cover the loose ends. When the piece of beading is finished there are several ways of finishing off the ends. One of the easiest ways is to weave the weft thread (without any beads) in and out of the warp threads for several rows. Another method is to sandwich the loose warp ends by gluing a piece of felt or leather either side. If you use strips of leather you could then punch holes in one end, attach a buckle to the other and you will have made a genuine Red Indian belt.

Florentine embroidery

If you have ever seen a piece of Florentine embroidery you might easily have thought it was a painting rather than a kind of tapestry worked with wool on canvas. Florentine work is also known as Bargello and is sometimes called Hungarian point. Florentine embroidery is simple and quick to do as you cover several holes in the canvas with one stitch, unlike conventional tapestry work using petit point or gros point stitches. The finished result depends a great deal on a careful selection of colours. Traditional Florentine work is usually worked in different shades of the same basic colour, ranging in tone from dark to light.

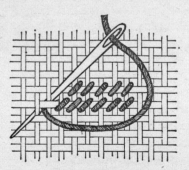

It is a good idea to work a small sample before you embark on a lengthy project.

When you explore Florentine work further you will come across patterns with names such as Flame, Honeycomb, Brick, Gothic, Trellis and Diamond. They are all fairly simple and as long as you follow the design charts carefully you will soon find that you have built up quite a large 'library' of stitches. Charts are worked out on graph paper. Each square represents a hole in the canvas, so you can see exactly how many holes each stitch should cover. Nearly all patterns are symmetrical. Once you have worked one row, the 'foundation row', the rest should fall into place quite easily. You will find lots of useful ways to use your finished pieces – as cushion covers, belts, trimmings for clothes, chair covers, mats and bags.

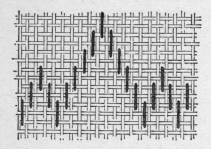 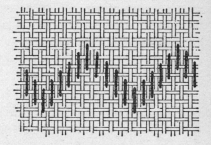

Shoulder bag

To make a simple shoulder bag you will need a piece of canvas 4 cm (1½ in) wider than the finished width of the bag, and twice the length you want the bag to be. Tape all the edges with wide Sellotape before you start. This will stop them from fraying and catching as you work. We suggest you start by using a simple zigzag or flame design in order to gain confidence. Take care to count out the first row accurately and then the rest will be easy! When you have finished one row start the next with a different colour. You should always work from left to right – unless you are left-handed. Always bring your needle out at the front and back of the work at the end of each stitch. If you try to do the stitch in one movement the canvas soon gets stretched. It is better not to start with a knot as this makes the back of the canvas bulky.

However, you must weave the loose ends in as you go along.

When you have finished the embroidery attach a lining to the two shorter ends by putting the right sides together and using a small back stitch (use the holes in the canvas to help you). Again with the right sides together sew up the sides of your bag taking the lining in as well. Turn the bag right side out. You can make a strap by plaiting several strands of wool together and sewing this firmly to the sides of the bag.

Berlin work

Canvas tapestry work is a form of embroidery which has its roots in the great tradition of tapestry works with which walls in medieval manors were hung. Canvas embroidery differs from most other forms of embroidery in that the *whole* of the fabric is covered, rather than the design only being worked into part of it. Berlin work is a form of canvas embroidery which spread throughout Europe and into America during the 19th century. Before this time people had created their own designs, rather like making their own paintings.

In 1804 a Berlin print-seller began to distribute coloured needlework designs on squared paper. From these designs anyone could copy the picture on to squared canvas and so make their own tapestries. It was very much like the introduction of 'painting-by-numbers' kits in more modern times. Not surprisingly these designs were immensely popular and it is estimated that 14,000 different designs were produced in Europe and imported into Britain in the next thirty years, despite the fact that some of the original designs cost as much as £40! This would be at least five times as much in present day money. One or two of these designs have been reproduced by the Victoria and Albert Museum in London.

The name 'Berlin work' came not from the prints but from the wools which were used to embroider the pictures. The wool was made in a part of Germany called Gotha and dyed in strong, bright colours in Berlin.

If you have ever done any tapestry work, you have probably used a printed canvas. Making up and transferring your own design to canvas embroidery is certainly much nearer to a real craft than some people would imagine.

To make the design you will need sheets of squared graph paper, which you can get from stationers, a pencil or pen and coloured pencils or felt-tip pens. To embroider from your design you will need a double-thread canvas, which is called Penelope, presumably after the wife of Ulysses who refused to give him up as dead until she had completed her tapestry work. These canvases are by no means cheap nowadays and nor are the tapestry wools, although you can use the finer (3- or at most 4-ply) knitting wools and crêpe wools which are cheaper. Canvas and special tapestry wools have to be bought in a specialist needlework shop. So, if Berlin work interests you, you might have to start with a special investment of Christmas or birthday money. The assistants in needlework shops are usually knowledgeable about their materials and willing to give you advice about the quantities and qualities of wool you will need. Take your design along and ask them to help you.

One further word before we embark on the detailed instructions. Long before the world became conscious of the need to avoid male and female roles, and at a time when men were even more concerned with 'manly' pursuits than they are now, many men were tapestry-making enthusiasts, and continue to be so. So do not think of this as women's work!

Designing your Berlin work

Decide what you want to make. We suggest that you start with something reasonably small. There is nothing more discouraging at the start of a new venture than not finishing your first piece of work. We have chosen to use a small portrait of the family cat, Mao, which could be framed or could be made into a small cushion.

First make an outline drawing of your picture on plain paper. Indicate the colour areas on the drawing. Then transfer your picture to the graph paper, adjusting the shape to fit within the squares. Colour it in square by square. We cannot use colour here and in fact many of the original designs were printed in black and white, using a code for the colours as we have. Berlin wool had many, many shades and tones of each colour which faded into each

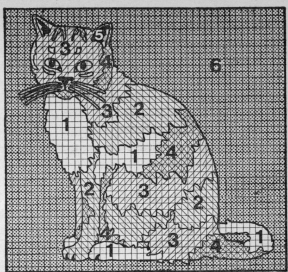

Key	Colour
1	WHITE
2	ORANGE
3	LIGHT BROWN
4	DARK BROWN
5	BLACK
6	GREEN

other. In 1840 a Miss Lambert commented in her *Handbook of Embroidery* that there were 'at least twelve distinct hues of green and every one of these has perhaps twenty gradations of tint'. Try to produce this effect in your work too.

Preparing your canvas

Now you are ready to begin the embroidery, copying it stitch by stitch, square by square from your design. You will find your pattern much easier to follow if you mark the heavier lines on your graph paper, which often appear at ten-square intervals, on to the canvas also at ten-square intervals.

The stitches

There are a number of stitches which you can use on canvas. We start you off here with the two most basic and common.

Tent stitch or petit point. This is the simplest canvas stitch and has the advantage that it can go up, across or diagonally on the canvas.

When you are sewing on canvas, always bring the needle through a hole in the canvas to start the stitch and go down through a hole in the next row to finish the stitch. Work every row from left to right (or, if you are left-handed right to left) so that all the stitches go in the same direction.

Tent stitch or petit point is better for detailed work and finer canvases, cross stitch which we describe next is for larger background areas and coarser canvases.

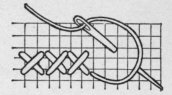

Cross stitch. This is a very good stitch to use for Berlin work and for following a diagram, as each completed stitch can easily be seen to represent one square on the diagram. It is also economical and gives a good finish to the back of the work. Follow the same general rules as for tent stitch and add one more – always have the top stitches going in the same direction.

Things to make

Here are a few ideas which you might like to consider. Cover a small cardboard box by making a paper pattern for the top and sides of the box and embroidering the canvas to this shape. Glue the canvas to the box top and sides, turning in a narrow (1-cm or $\frac{1}{4}$-in) edge of unworked canvas all round. The pattern given here is for making the cardboard box itself.

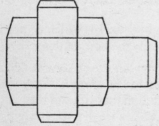

Bookmarks, belts, spectacle cases, change purses, and pin cushions are all small and simple to make. Leave about 2 cm ($\frac{3}{4}$ in) of unworked canvas around the edges to fold in. For a belt and a bookmark you will need to oversew the edges through both thicknesses to give a firm border.

2 Using colour and cloth

Appliqué and fabric collage

Appliqué is the French word for 'applied'. It is a method of
embroidery in which the design or picture is made by applying
(or fixing) one fabric to another. A collage is a method of
picture-making which uses shapes and textures rather than lines
and paint. In most collage work the materials which are applied to
the background are glued down. In appliqué work the materials
are sewn one to another. But in making fabric collages you have the
choice of stitching or gluing, so that appliqué work is also a part of
making fabric collage pictures.

Appliqué

First plan your design on paper. Keep your early efforts simple so
that you can concentrate on acquiring the skill before you go on to
more complicated designs. Transfer the outline of your design on
to your background material. Use a charcoal pencil on light colours
and chalk on dark colours.

For appliqué work you need lightweight materials which do not
fray too easily. Cotton materials are really the best, both for the
base and the bits which are applied to it.

Cut out the shapes which you are going to sew to the background,
making them 1 cm ($\frac{1}{2}$ in) larger all round so that you can turn under
the edges before sewing them down. Make sure that the straight
threads of the fabric run in the same direction as the straight
threads of the background cloth. This will help to make sure that
the materials lie flat, one against the other.

Now fold in the turnings all round the pieces to the wrong side,
and tack them in position with small running stitches.

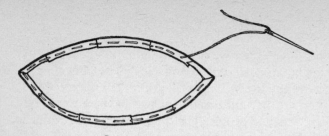

Where you are working with round or irregular shapes you will have to snip or nick the turnings so that they will lie down flat.

Tack the pieces on to your main material, making sure that you match the straight threads of both the backcloth and the pieces. Hem the pieces on to the backcloth with small neat hemming stitches or with a small running stitch just in from the edges. Remove the tacking threads carefully so that the material doesn't gather up.

You can decorate your appliqué work further with embroidery stitches, possibly outlining the pieces or embroidering patterns on to them. You can also appliqué small pieces on top of larger pieces.

African appliqué

The appliqué work we have described so far is the work of Europe, using fine and often expensive cloths and minute stitches. In Africa the appliqué work is cruder and less delicate, but often more expressive and lively. It is a skilled craft in Dahomey in West Africa where they make wall hangings and banners covered with animals, birds and people. The creatures are often symbolic, representing characteristics, like courage and pride, or telling proverbs. The banners were a way of recording history just as the Bayeux tapestry recorded the Norman invasion of England in 1066.

Build up your picture from the shapes you have in your scrap bag. You can use materials with a looser weave and a heavier weight for this sort of appliqué, as you do not need to turn in the edges, but can overstitch any frayed bits (see page 9). Add one shape to another to give your creatures legs, wings, and ears etc.

Place your pieces on the backcloth and move them around to suit your sense of design. Don't sew them down until you have made your whole picture work together. It might be about a visit to the zoo, about the school playground, about a market or the country in autumn, or it might be a gathering of memories from your holidays. Tack the pieces in position on the backcloth and sew them on using cross stitch, blanket stitch, chain stitch or overstitch (see pages 8–10).

Panamanian cut-work pictures

In Central America the San Blas Indians of Panama have a completely different form of appliqué work in which the uppermost of two layers of cloth is cut away to reveal the colour of the layer beneath. They devised this type of embroidery to decorate the yokes of their loose blouses, but they now make all sorts of decorations. To start you need one dark and one light piece of material the size you want your picture to be. Use firm cotton cloth like poplin. You don't want it too thick as you have to sew through two or more layers quite often. You also need scraps of very bright materials, usually plain but they could be patterned, and your scissors, needle and thread, and a piece of chalk with which to draw your patterns. Draw the design on the piece of dark cloth. Tack the dark cloth, which will be the top layer, on to the light piece, taking care not to tack across the part of the design that you will want to cut away. Then carefully cut out the design, e.g. the snake and the plants and the border in our picture, to reveal the cloth underneath. The two cloth layers should still be held together by the tacking.

If you want to add bits of a third or fourth colour, say on the flowers around the snake, add them now. Slip scraps of cloth in behind the bits you have cut from the dark layer. Pin them in position. Make sure that these scraps are large enough to fill the space when the edges of the dark cloth are turned back for hemming.

Now, at last, you are ready to sew. Turn in the edges of the outlines, making the areas of lighter colour which show through

as wide or as narrow as you wish. If you have a coloured piece slipped in, sew through all the thicknesses. Hem neatly along the turned edges of the cuts to fix the pieces firmly in position.

Here is an example of an original picture of a dragonlike creature made by a San Blas Indian woman. The artist who made it used orange, green, pink, red and blue behind the stripes on the dragon and in the background. The main outline and border are left white.

Fabric collage

When you are working on a fabric collage you need to have a good selection of different textured materials to express different things in your picture. Try to collect together as many different sorts of material as you can – plain and patterned, felt, lightweight tweed, corduroy, seersucker, net, scraps of tapestry canvas, nylon fur, lamé or lurex. You can use other materials too, like vilene and scraps of soft leather. You can expand your ideas by using buttons, sequins and beads, lace, ric-rac braid, piping cord, string, embroidery threads and wool, feathers, snap fasteners and tinsel. There is really no limit to what you can use so long as the material suits your subject and you can fix it satisfactorily to your backcloth.

You can either sew the pieces to the background (as we have already described) or you can use glue. You can use clear, cellulose paste, but what we call impact adhesives stick faster and firmer. Clear Bostick, Evostick and Copydex are suitable. When you are buying your glue, look carefully at the maker's advice on the box or tube to see if it suits your purpose. Use glue sparingly, especially near the edges of the pieces or it will run out and get messy.

You need a firm backing cloth for your fabric picture. If you are only using glue for fixing and not doing any sewing, you should fix your backing cloth to a board first. A piece of firm cardboard or a piece of hardboard is suitable. Let the glue dry well, making sure the cloth lies really flat before you start making your picture. If you are sewing on some or all of the materials, you will have to mount your collage when it is completed.

Play around with your pieces of material against the backing cloth, moving them from place to place, overlapping some, contrasting colours and textures. It often seems better to get inspiration from the existing shape of pieces rather than trying to cut cloth to suit your needs. Once you have decided how you are going to build up the picture, and in which order you are going to apply the pieces (main background pieces first, foreground later and details at the end), take the pieces off the backcloth, but try to keep them in order in a box so the right piece will be ready to hand when you want to use it.

There are various ways of fixing the pieces to the background. You can use all or any of them in one picture.

1 Use the method described in appliqué work.

2 Where you want to have a rougher outline, or where the fabric has a very secure edge which will not fray, sew straight round the edge without turning it under. Alternatively you can sew through the actual material if you want to outline the piece. Decide whether you want to use a contrasting or matching colour for your stitching. Vary your stitches to get different effects.

3 Use glue.

Pieces can be laid on top of each other both to build up the details and to give depth contrast in your picture. For instance, you might stick on a patch of corduroy to represent the walls of a log cabin and then sew felt windows on to the corduroy. You could build up a street by putting one building on top of another to give perspective.

Experiment with all sorts of different effects. You can see what they will look like by laying the pieces on the backcloth before you fix them down.

Here are some ideas to get you thinking.

1 Unravel the edges of a loosely woven material to make a shaggy creature or landscape.

2 Use a scrap of floral cloth in a flower-bed.

3 Use the fine-woven string bag which citrus fruits are packed in.

4 Embroider details and textures on to larger pieces to show the sun's rays, rain, flowers, features etc.

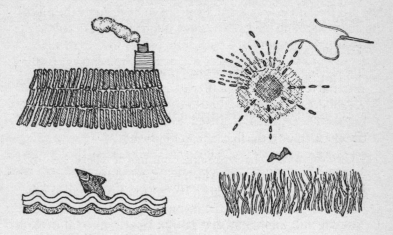

5 Build up fine cloth or net to make a sunset.

6 Produce special effects by tie-dyeing pieces of material. You could produce a stormy sky by marbling your backcloth with the crumple dye method (see page 40–1).

7 Thatch a roof or make a fence with string.

8 Use felt-tip pens to add details like features and whiskers.

9 Use cotton wool for snow and beards. Try colouring it with paint, ink and dyes.

10 Use layers of ric-rac braid for water.

11 Use frayed out wool for hair and manes.

12 Cut flowers and trees out of a large-patterned material.

Tie-dyeing

Tie-dyeing is the art of putting patterns on cloth by tying the material so parts of the cloth will take dye and other parts will not. As children we used to admire an exquisite mauve silk shawl of our mother's, light as a cobweb and sprinkled with dots and circles of colour. This is the finest bit of tie-dyeing I have ever seen, made far away in India by craftsmen with immense skill and patience. It would be wonderful to reproduce work like that, but even for the beginner tie-dyeing can produce some very satisfactory results.

To start with we suggest that you use lightweight cotton cloth which will be easy to handle and will take the dye well. Avoid drip-dry materials which resist dye, like specially treated poplins. Man-made fibres, like nylon, are difficult to work with too. Use white and light-coloured fabrics. Ask for a bit of an old sheet for your first experiments and, even when you gain experience, always ask if it is all right for you to dye the chosen bit of material or piece of clothing.

You will need to buy some cold water dyes, perhaps using two or more colours on one piece of cloth. You need to weigh your material when it is dry to find out how much dye you will need. You should follow the instructions on the tin to get the best results.

The tying

There are many ways to tie material to get many different effects. We start off by showing the well-known sunburst pattern to explain the principles. Further ideas come later on.

Hold the cloth by the point which you want to have as the centre of the sunburst. Let the cloth drop down evenly from this point. Tie the cloth as tightly as you can in various places. Use thin string where you want fine lines on the cloth and heavier string, tape or raffia where you want broader bands. You can also tie cloth with ordinary sewing thread, knitting wool or rubber bands.

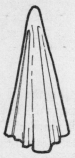  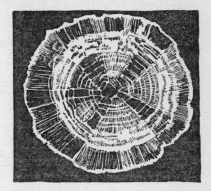

The dyeing

Take great care when working with dye that you don't splash it anywhere – for, of course, it will dye whatever it touches! Put newspaper on the floor, cover your clothes with an apron and have a cloth ready to mop up any splashes. You may wish to wear rubber gloves, for although the dye will wash off your hands, it can get into your nails.

Prepare the dye according to the instructions on the tin. Wet the article in warm water so that it will be better prepared to absorb the dye water. Put the article in the dye bath and stir with a wooden spoon or smooth stick to make sure that the dye gets to all parts of the material. Leave it to soak for as long as instructed, but for at least an hour.

Lift the cloth out of the dye bath and rinse it with several changes of cold water. Some of the dye will run away when you do this, but the water will soon begin to clear.

Remove the string or other ties very carefully. Wet knots are difficult to undo, so if you use scissors be very careful not to snip the cloth too. Now you can admire the effect of your work.

Remember how you tied the cloth so that you can repeat the pattern if you wish. In this way you will build up your knowledge of possible patterns. Now soak the cloth in hot soapy water for a further five minutes. You do this to ensure that the dye is really fast and won't come out in future washes. Rinse it again and hang it up to dry.

You may want to re-tie the cloth and dye it again with a different colour. Again you will learn from experience how to get the best effects in combining colours. Dye with the second colour in the same way as you did with the first.

Other ways of tying

As we have said there are many different effects to be gained from different methods of tying the cloth. Think carefully about what you want to use your cloth for and so what sort of patterns you want to make and where you want the pattern to be.

Tying around pebbles or seeds

Gather a collection of pebbles or large seeds. Make sure that you wash all the pebbles completely clean. Tie them into your cloth like little mushrooms, then dye the cloth as described above.

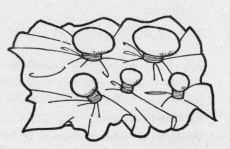

You can get a great variety
of patterns in this manner.

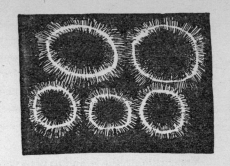

Tying in knots

You can get various effects by tying knots in the material itself.
Fold the cloth lengthways. Roll it up into a long tube. Tie knots
in it as firmly as possible. Dye the cloth. Later try other ways of
knotting the cloth.

Marbling

This form of tie-dyeing is used widely in both East and West
Africa. It creates an all-over effect of clouds or turbulent water
rather than a definite pattern as the other methods do.

Crumple your material up into a ball as tightly as you can. Light
materials are most suitable so that you can squash the ball as
tightly as possible. Wrap string round the ball in several directions

to hold the ball together. You can use wide elastic
bands for this too and they are easier to manage.

Dye your cloth ball in the usual way. This method
of dyeing lends itself to double or even treble
dyeing so that you get two or three colours of
marbling mixed across each other.

Twist and tie

You really need a friend to help you prepare your material for this
type of dyeing.

Each of you take one end of the cloth. One of you twists the
material as if you were trying to squeeze water out of it. Twist it so
tight that the material doubles over on itself. Tie it tightly in this
position. Dye the material in the usual way. This will give you
material with a wavy-lined pattern across the cloth.

Folding

Fold your piece of material in half lengthways. Then fold it again
like a concertina or fan. Fix the folds in position by sewing a
thread through at the top and bottom. Tie the material and dye it.
This method will give a stripy effect.

Sewing the pattern into the cloth

Make an outline of the pattern you want on the cloth with a
charcoal pencil (this is better than an ordinary one because it will
wash off more easily!). Sew using a running stitch or basting stitch
along these lines. When you have sewn in all the threads, pull both
ends of each thread to gather the material together and tie them off.

Dye the material in the usual way. The lines of stitches will be reproduced on the material.

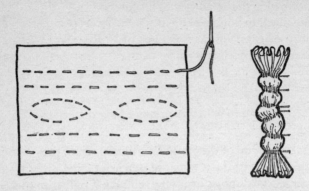

Indonesian Batik

Batik uses the same principle of dyeing as tie-dyeing does – that is, blocking out part of the material so it will not take the dye. With batik it is a layer of wax which protects the cloth from the colour.

Batik is a very old method of making patterns on cloth. It probably developed in the East and is certainly widely practised in Indonesia. It is estimated that 40,000,000 metres (44,000,000 yds) of cloth are dyed there every year by this method! In Nigeria in West Africa there is another form of batik in which starch paste is used to resist the dye. This cloth, almost always dyed dark blue with indigo, is called *adire* which means 'to take, to tie, and to dye'. This name covers all types of cloth produced in that area which are dyed with parts of them protected from the colour. The method of batik we explain here uses wax rather than starch. Probably you will never be able to match the skill of the great African craftswomen, but many of your results will be beautiful and all will be fascinating to do. The materials you will need for your batik work are:

Paraffin wax like that used for candle-making. If you can afford a mixture of beeswax and paraffin wax you will find it more flexible, but it is more expensive and you will do very well with paraffin wax alone. Just as when you make candles, you need to be careful when you melt down wax. It becomes *very* hot and can scald you badly if you are not sensible. Always turn the pan handles away from the edge of the stove where you may knock against them.

Paint brushes. These are for painting the hot wax on to the material. Collect together an assortment of brushes for doing both broad stretches and finer work. Don't use good brushes because the wax will ruin them – cheap ones are perfectly satisfactory. You may like to have a charcoal pencil to draw your planned design on to the cloth.

Kerosene for removing the wax from the cloth after the dyeing.

A *cold water dye* and the materials recommended for dyeing on the tin.

The rest of the equipment you need can be found in most kitchens: two saucepans (one should fit into the other), foil, an electric iron, newspaper, paper towels or absorbent paper, and a few drawing pins are useful.

Use cotton cloth and, as with tie-dye, avoid crease-resistant materials which also resist dye. If you use man-made fibres like nylon make sure that you use a specially prepared cold dye for that sort of material.

Preparing the cloth

Pin your cloth out on a board or table to keep it flat while you work. Draw your design on the cloth with a charcoal pencil, which will wash out easily. You may like to plan it first on paper and copy it from the paper. Decide which areas you want to keep from the dye.

Preparing and laying on the wax

Make a 'double boiler' out of the two saucepans, putting one on top of the other with water in the lower one. Put a sheet of foil between the two pans and leave some foil sticking out all round to catch any wax drips. Wax is very inflammable and you must be careful when you melt it.

Heat the water in the bottom pan. Put the wax in the top pan over the heat so that it melts. You need to get it to reach a temperature

of 170°F (75°C) and a kitchen sugar thermometer would be useful
to measure this. Remove the saucepan from the heat and laying the
cloth flat, paint the wax on to the parts of your design which you
want to stay undyed. If the wax is absorbed by the fabric it will
spread. Let the wax dry while you prepare the dye according to the
instructions on the tin.

Immerse the cloth in the dye bath gently so that the wax doesn't
crack too much. Leave it for twenty minutes or longer according
to the instructions with the dye. Now rinse the material
thoroughly in warm water. Hang the cloth out to dry.

Remember whenever you are using dye that splashes of colour will
mark whatever they fall on. Cover the work top and floor around
with newspaper. Mop up any drops, and wear rubber gloves if you
want to keep your nails looking normal!

When the cloth is dry, scrape off any excess wax. (You can use it
again.) Lay a pad of newspaper on your ironing table. Put a layer
of paper towels or other absorbent paper over it. Now iron with a
hot iron. The heat of the iron will melt the wax which will be
absorbed by the paper. Replace the paper towels from time to
time as they get saturated with wax. Iron the cloth all over, not
just on the waxed parts, for the heat of the iron will also help to
fix the dye.

Now your work is ready to be admired. But it may not be complete,
for you might be using a second or third colour. The wax this
time could be put on to block out the first colour, allowing the dye
to colour the white spaces if you leave them wax free. You can, of
course, leave the first lot of wax and add more for the second
dyeing.

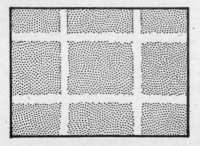 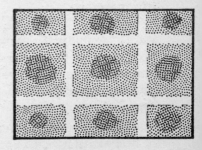

On the previous page is a very simple example of how waxing different parts of a cloth in two separate dyeing sessions will produce colours on the cloth. The first lot of wax, which covers the white lines, has been left on after the first dye bath. The squares were filled at the second waxing, leaving the circles to take the second colour.

Marbled effect

If you want to get an all over marbled effect on the cloth, brush a thin layer of wax over the whole piece of cloth. Let it dry. Crumple up the piece of material so that the wax cracks in irregular lines. Dye the material in the usual way. The dye will take where the wax has cracked, producing whirls and splashes of colour.

Making Rag Rugs

When we were children in Canada we had French Canadian rag rugs made in Quebec which were decorated with the symbol of Canada, the autumn-tinted maple leaf. To the North American settlers, as to many other people who faced poverty and few resources, rag rugs were a way of re-using something worn out and creating out of it something useful – and artistic.

The rags were stored and collected for this purpose throughout the year. Today we have a quicker source of collection – the jumble sale. For a pound or so you can probably pick up several cotton dresses matching the planned colour of your design. Wash them, cut them up and you have your 'rags'.

For rag rug making you need a very simple loom made up of a base board, an upright, and nails to hold the work in position. You make the rug in long strips on this loom and then sew the strips together to form the rug.

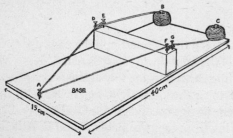

Stand balls of string on nails B and C, which act as 'feeders'. Run lengths of string from B and C, making a figure of eight around D and E, and F and G. Tie the ends round A. This forms the warp of the loom.

Now prepare your rags. Tear your cloth into strips not more than 2 cm ($\frac{3}{4}$ in) wide and as long as you can make them. Use a piece of card to cut these strips quickly into equal lengths. Take some card about 20 cm (8 in) long and 6 cm ($2\frac{1}{2}$ in) wide. Fold it in half lengthwise. Wrap a strip of cloth round it in a single layer.

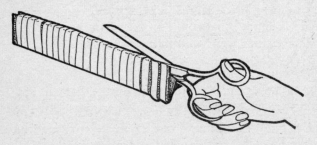

Cut along the open edge. You now have your rag strips ready to knot on to the warp thread of your loom.

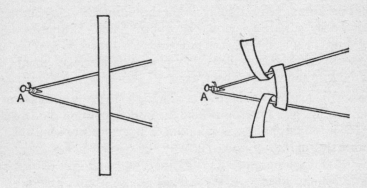

Wrap each strip over the warp threads and pull the ends up between the warps. Slide the knot down towards nail A. Knot each strip on in this way, sliding them down firmly against each other until the warp is too full to tie the knots tightly on it. Now lift the string from nail A, loosen the figures of eight on D–E and F–G, and draw a length of string from the two spools, B and C. Attach the last knot you have made to nail A and refix the warp threads to the small nails again, keeping the warp tight. Now you can continue to knot on to the adjusted thread.

Once you have made a strip about a metre long, you can begin to coil it up and sew it together to make the centre of your rug. You can make either an oval rug or a circular one. You start your centre accordingly. For an oval rug the central strip should be a bit less than half the length of the final rug you want to make.

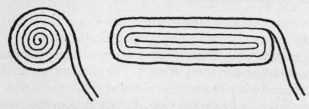

Sew the strips together with strong thread. Button thread is the most suitable. Ease the strips round the curves so that the fringed side will lie flat. Do not cut off the warp threads until you have completed your rug to the size you want. Then cut off the warp threads and tie them tightly behind the last knot. Sew the end of the strip into the back of the rug.

You can mix the colours you use in your rug completely which will give a speckled effect. You can concentrate on one colour, using a mixture of different shades and tones. You can do strips in one colour for some distance and then change to another colour. We recommend that you start with a fairly small rug and then as your skill increases work upwards in size.

Braided or plaited rugs

Another type of rag rug can be made by plaiting or braiding long, flat strips of material and then sewing them together. This makes a flatter, smoother surface than the rag loom rug. Braided rugs are more suitable for a bathroom, kitchen hall or playroom; rag loom rugs are more suitable for a bedroom or hearthside.

Braided rugs can be made with cotton or wool scraps or with a firm cotton base woven together with wool scraps. As you are working with a continuous strip of braiding, you have to keep joining the strips of cloth together. You do this as you work, because you don't want to have to work with strips longer than a metre in length or you'll begin to get in a tangle. It is important to keep the strips as flat as possible, so join the strips 'on the bias', and to keep the mat surface smooth, you turn the strips over at the edge.

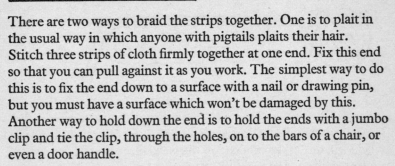

There are two ways to braid the strips together. One is to plait in the usual way in which anyone with pigtails plaits their hair. Stitch three strips of cloth firmly together at one end. Fix this end so that you can pull against it as you work. The simplest way to do this is to fix the end down to a surface with a nail or drawing pin, but you must have a surface which won't be damaged by this. Another way to hold down the end is to hold the ends with a jumbo clip and tie the clip, through the holes, on to the bars of a chair, or even a door handle.

Now start plaiting. Pass the left-hand strip over the centre strip. Pass the right-hand strip over the centre strip. Continue like this until you have made a strip as long as you need.

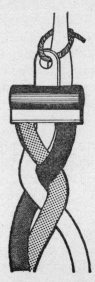

The other method is best if you are using a mixture of cotton and wool material, as it covers the cotton base with the wool. Sew your strip of wool cloth to the centre of a long strip of cotton cloth so it falls away from it at right angles. Wrap it once round the base strip so that it lies firmly between the two cotton strips.

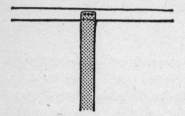 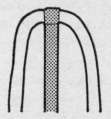

Wrap the central strip of material round the right hand strip, passing it under and over that strip. Pass it under the left hand strip, then back over the left hand strip, and under and over the right hand strip. Continue in this way so that you weave the two cotton strips together and cover them with the wool strip.

 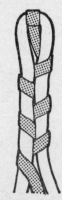

Join the braided strips together in the same way as you joined the rag loom strips, depending on whether you want a round or an oval rug, sewing about a metre of braid into the rug each time. Use button thread for strength.

Using the first, straight braiding or plaiting, method you can have a rug which is multi-coloured throughout or you can work with different shades of one colour (dark, medium and light). It is, of course easier to collect rags for a completely multi-coloured rug as you can use everything that comes your way. If you want particular shades and tones you will have to search out the right colours. But the occasional attendance at jumble sales will probably produce all you need quite cheaply.

For the second, wrap over weave, method you can again make a random coloured mat or you can work several rows in one colour so that you make a rug in bands of contrasting colours.

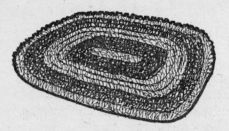

3 Using wool and string

Macramé

If you are good at tying useful knots you will find the 'decorative' art of knotting almost as easy. From studying historical records, paintings and actual fragments of ancient knot work we can tell that even cavemen were expert in using knots for hunting and fishing. The Egyptians were more creative than practical and developed the skill for using knots to decorate their clothes. Sailors are well known for their skills in the craft of knotting, and were largely responsible for spreading the art of macramé around the world.

Today people are rediscovering the craft of macramé, and you can see examples ranging from huge brightly coloured wall hangings, plant holders and bottle covers, to fringing on clothes, belts, bags, mats, cushions, rugs, and even whole garments.

If you would like to try your hand at macramé all you will need to start is a piece of fairly soft board, or a firm bolster-shaped cushion, two long pins, – preferably with T-shaped ends to stop the thread from slipping off – and some strong string or piping cord.

We will tell you how to do the two basic knots and once you have mastered just these two knots and their variations you will be able to make any number of useful things – belts, bags, lampshades, screens, and if you feel really adventurous you could make a hammock!

It is a good idea to experiment with a sampler (a collection of the different knots you can do) to begin with. This will give you a chance to practise all the different knots without feeling that you have to finish anything!

Pin a length of string, 15–25 cm (6–10 in) long on to your board. This is called the 'foundation'. The threads which you attach to the foundation thread are the ones you will be working with, and as a rough guide they should be eight times the length of your proposed piece of work (or four times when doubled). The first diagram shows how to 'set on' the threads using a reversed half-hitch knot.

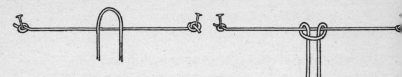

The first of the basic knots is the 'half-hitch'. To work the knot from the left, hold the right-hand thread of the pair taut, pass the left-hand thread over and under the right-hand one, and through the loop as shown.

When you have practised the left hand half-hitch several times, try holding the left-hand thread taut and pass the right-hand thread over and under (in the same way as before). Now you can try alternating the two knots to make a chain or 'see-saw knot'. Yet another variation is to use two threads (a pair) at a time making a 'double half-hitch'.

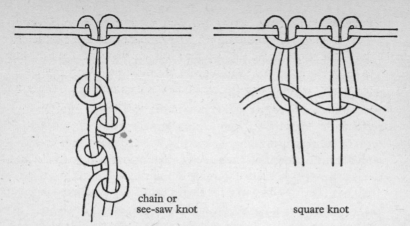

chain or
see-saw knot

square knot

The other basic knot is the 'flat knot', known by sailors as the 'square knot'. To practise this knot you will have to set two threads on to your foundation thread, thus making four threads in all. The middle two threads are known as the 'filler core'. Pass the left-hand thread under the filler core and over the right-hand thread. Now pass the right-hand thread over the filler core and back under the left-hand thread, through the loop you have made, from front to back. If you forget which thread to use, the one that has just come under the filler core always goes over next. The picture shows this knot at the half-way stage.

If you want to make something whilst you practise the knots, why not make a necklace, using either the see-saw knot, or a combination of knots. Use fairly thick smooth string or piping cord, and remember to cut the threads eight times the length you want your finished necklace to be. When the knotting is finished take it off the board and knot the ends to stop the necklace from un-knotting itself! You could try creating different effects by using different coloured threads, and incorporating beads into your work. Instead of setting your threads on to a foundation thread you can set them straight on to a buckle for a belt.

Crochet

Crochet comes from the French word 'croche' meaning hook.
It was probably invented by French nuns in the sixteenth century.
The nuns were greatly impressed by the beautiful macramé work
the sailors were doing on their long voyages and bringing into
port, and tried to copy the intricate patterns. In their efforts to
recreate the complicated knots the sailors used they developed a
form of knitting using a hook, and this was crochet! Many years
later the nuns passed on their secrets to the poor people in Ireland
during the terrible years of famine in the 1840s. Since then the
Irish have been well known for their beautifully crocheted lace.

It isn't difficult to learn to crochet, and crocheting has many
advantages over knitting! You only have one hook to carry around
with you, and there is never a problem with dropped stitches.
Once you have learned the basic stitches, and their abbreviations
(in order to follow a pattern), you will be surprised at the great
variety of things you can make.

When you are learning the stitches it is better to use a fairly large
crochet hook and thick wool.

Holding the wool and hook

Hold the hook in your right hand in the same way as you hold a
pencil, with your thumb and first finger fairly near the hook end.
The wool goes over the first and second fingers of your left hand,
under the third, and loosely round the little finger. The thumb and
first finger hold the work as it is made.

Making a chain

All crochet stitches are based on the action of pulling one loop
through another. Nearly all crochet work begins with a length of
chain stitches which form the foundation. Make a slip knot in the
end of your wool, and put the end of your crochet hook through it.
Hold the wool between the thumb and first finger of your left hand.
Pass the hook from left to right under the wool on your left hand,
and catching the loop you have formed with the hook pull it
through the loop already on the hook. This is an important step,
and is known as wool round hook (wrh). Carry on making loops
and pulling them through thus making a long single chain.

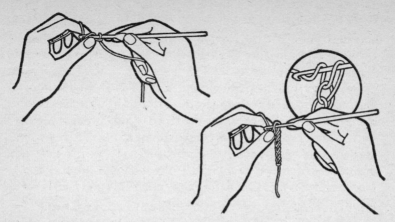

Slip stitch (sl st)

Make a length of basic chain. Put the hook through the last stitch made. As you will be working from left to right, this stitch will be to the left of the hook. Put the wool round the hook (wrh) as before and pull the loop formed through both the stitches on the hook. (Now there is only one stitch on the hook.)

Double crochet (dc)

Make a length of basic chain. Put the hook through the second stitch to the left in the chain. Put the wool round the hook and pull the loop through the first stitch on the hook (two stitches on the hook). Put the wool round the hook again, but this time pull the loop through both stitches.

Always begin a row of double crochet on the second stitch, as the first stitch is known as the turning chain and gives your work the right amount of depth. You should also remember on the second row that your hook should go through *both* loops of the stitch below.

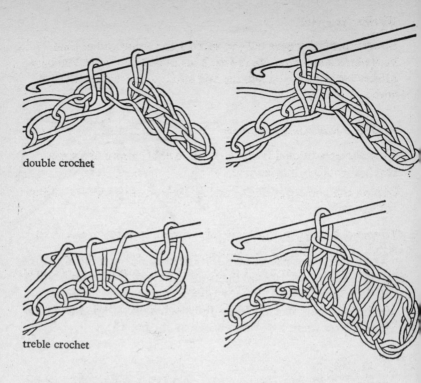

double crochet

treble crochet

Treble crochet (tr)

Make a basic chain. Pass the wool round the hook and into the
fourth stitch in the chain (three stitches on hook). Pass the wool
round the hook again and pull through only two stitches on the
hook (two stitches on hook). Pass the wool round the hook again
and pull through the remaining two loops. Treble crochet needs
three chain stitches between each row to act as a turning chain.

Long treble (ltr)

Make a basic chain. Pass the wool round the hook twice, and put
the hook through the sixth stitch in the basic chain, pass the wool
round the hook and pull through one stitch (four stitches on
hook). Pass the wool round the hook and pull through another two
loops. Put the wool round the hook again and pull through the
remaining two loops. This stitch needs a turning chain of five
stitches between rows.

Working in rounds

Many crochet patterns tell you to work in rounds rather than backwards and forwards in rows. This means that when you have made a basic chain you join the first stitch to the last with a slip stitch.

Making a traditional Irish daisy

To make a traditional Irish daisy follow this pattern using the stitches you have just learned.

Make a chain of ten stitches and join the ends together with a slip stitch.

1st round 3 ch, 35 tr, into ring, join with a slip stitch to the third stitch of the 3 ch at the beginning.

2nd round 6 ch, miss 2 tr, 1 tr on next *3 ch, miss 2 tr, 1 tr on next, repeat from * all the way round, 3 ch, join.

3rd round 1 dc, 1 tr, 3 ltr, 1 tr, 1 dc all into every space, join and fasten off.

Making crochet squares

You can either make the squares all in one colour, or change the colour for each separate round.

1st round Make a chain of five stitches, join with a slip stitch. 3 ch, 2 tr into circle, 2 ch making a corner, 3 tr into circle, 2 ch, 3 tr into circle. 2 ch, 3 tr into circle, 2 ch, join with a slip stitch to last stitch.

2nd round 3 tr into a space in the first round, 2 ch, 3 tr, 1 ch, this makes one corner so repeat three times to make the other corners.

57

3rd round To make the corner, 3 tr into a corner space in the previous round, 2 ch, 3 tr, 1 ch. To form a side, 3 tr, 1 ch. Repeat these corner and side stitches on each side of the square.

When you have made enough squares you could sew them together to make a tabard. Make eight lengths of chain, or double crochet, and attach them to the sides of the tabard. You could also make a fringe round the bottom by pulling lengths of wool through with your crochet hook and knotting them. This is done in the same way as 'setting on' threads for macramé work (page 52).

Weaving

Weaving is one of the oldest crafts we know about. Early man must have been very pleased with himself when he discovered, 7,000 years ago, that by interlacing twigs and pieces of grass together at right angles he could produce a new fabric to replace his animal skins and furs. We know that weaving had reached a fairly advanced stage in biblical times from the description of Jacob's coat of many colours in the Old Testament. From these early beginnings people all over the world have continued the craft, developing their own forms of loom and traditional patterns of weave. The Chinese were famous many thousands of years ago for their fine woven silk, whilst other eastern countries were known for their rich cloths, woven with real gold metal threads.

Much more recently, in medieval England, weavers joined together in organized groups known as guilds. The guilds made certain rules which their members had to obey. They were not allowed to weave by candlelight, or between Christmas Day and Purification Day. The motto of the Canterbury weavers was:

Fair warp and fitting woof,
Weave a web that bideth proof.

Weaving has come a long way from its humble beginnings. Nowadays huge looms work mechanically, and can produce millions of metres of cloth at great speed, with the minimum of help from man! However, people living in countries without these modern, mechanical looms continue to practise the craft using home-spun, hand-dyed yarns, and very basic looms. All that a loom need do is hold the warp threads (the lengthwise ones) taut and parallel so that the weft threads (those which cross the warp) can be easily interlaced.

The back-strap loom is a simple device used in countries such as Mexico, Africa and North America to weave traditional rugs, blankets, belts and bags. It consists of two beams which hold the stretched warp threads. One beam is attached to a tree, or any object that will not move! The other beam is attached to the weaver by means of a special belt.

You can make a very simple loom from a stiff piece of cardboard. The card should be about 30 cm by 40 cm (12 in by 16 in), which means that your finished weaving will be 25 cm by 35 cm (10 in by 14 in). This may be smaller than you need, but you can always sew the pieces together afterwards, and it is easier to work on a smaller piece of card. Make equally spaced slits directly opposite each other on the narrow ends of the card. These slits should be about 3 mm ($\frac{1}{8}$ in) deep. The slits should be between 3 mm ($\frac{1}{8}$ in) and 6 mm ($\frac{1}{4}$ in) apart. If the slits are wide apart the finished piece will be fairly loose weave, but if the warp threads are close together you will get a tight compact weave. Choose a strong yarn for the warp and make a knot in one end. Slide the knot into the first slit and continue to wind the warp thread round the cardboard loom, using the slits to keep the threads taut and evenly spaced.

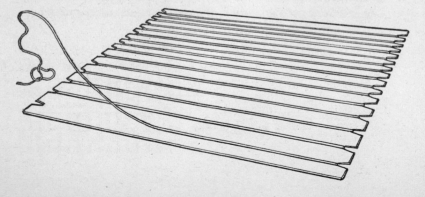

Thread a tapestry needle with a length of yarn and start weaving! The yarn should go over the first warp thread (leaving 8–10 cm, or 3–4 in, of yarn which can be darned in afterwards), under the second, over the third and so on to the last warp thread. The next row is made in the same way but you must go over the warp thread which you went under in the previous row, and under the one you went over.

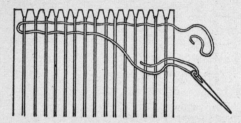

This simple darn-like weave is known as plain weave or tabby weave, and is only one of many different variations. Push each row of weft threads close up against each other, either with your fingers or a comb. This is known as 'beating' the weft, and will give your weaving an even appearance. When you need to start a new weft thread, leave an end hanging loose on this and the old weft thread that can be darned back in afterwards. Mechanical looms, and the larger hand looms, have a series of arms or harnesses which automatically raise the correct warp threads, creating a 'shed' for the weft to be passed through. The weaver literally throws the weft thread from side to side in a shuttle. If you find it difficult or tiring weaving your needle in and out every row, you could thread a ruler, or piece of dowel, over and under the warp threads. This would make a gap to pass the needle through. If you use two rulers, threaded in the reverse way to each other, you can leave one permanently in the warp and just thread in the second one for every other row.

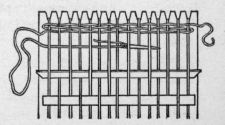

Try experimenting with different thicknesses of warp and weft threads. You can use strips of material instead of thread to give a really chunky weave. You can also introduce beads into your design by threading them on to the weft before beginning to weave.

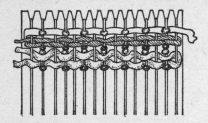

When you have made several pieces of cloth on your card loom, stitch them together to make a bag, belt, cushion cover or even a poncho, if you are very adventurous.

Italian bead curtains

In summer the doors of many Italian shops and houses are hung with bead curtains. This allows people and cool breezes to pass, but discourages insects and the dazzling sun. In Britain the dazzling sun is usually not such a problem, and nor, fortunately, are the insects. But bead curtains still give a Mediterranean air to a room or to a tall window.

For the 'beads' you can use brightly coloured wooden or glass beads, coloured drinking straws or macaroni. (Make sure that you buy macaroni which has holes through the centre and not spaghetti, which does not!)

Cut lengths of string longer than the drop of the door or window. Make a slip knot at the end of each strand and fix it on a drawing pin or small nail where it will be convenient for you to work. Thread the beads on to the strings – the long pieces of straw or macaroni should be separated with groups of beads or single beads. You can build up regular or random patterns along the strings.

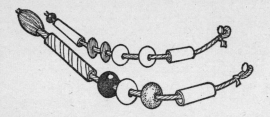

You can tie knots between beads or straws to vary the pattern and texture, but you will need to remember to make the string long enough for this. It is a good idea to have a large group of beads (say four or five) or one or two heavier beads at the bottom of each thread to hold it down.

The beads should be fairly close together but not too tightly packed or the curtain won't swing easily when you push through it. Tie a knot underneath or around the last bead to hold all the beads in place. Hang the lengths of beads from a row of drawing pins over the door or window and your curtain is complete.

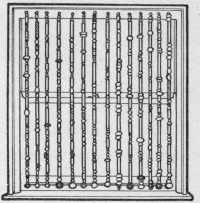

Wool pictures

The first wool pictures we saw were in a large new hotel. They were, in fact, mostly modern reproductions based on another nineteenth-century craft of the sea. These wool pictures usually depicted a single ship (possibly the one in which the artist sailed) but they sometimes showed a patriotic array of flags, a battle or a fleet of ships.

They were originally worked on bits of canvas sailcloth from which the sails, the hammocks and the sailors' kit-bags were made. They were sewn in thick wool using a combination of long and short stitch and rows of very long single stitches. The wool embroidery completely covered the canvas beneath. The long stitches stretched from one side of an area like a sail to the other, each 'stitch' held in position by the row above and below. The sails on these pictures were sometimes 'billowed' out with a layer of padding. In the old pictures the artist occasionally used a cuttlefish pen (like those we give to cage birds) to pad out the sail. The rigging was sewn over the main embroidery stitches with dark thread – again sometimes a very long stitch was used so that a single thread of 'rigging' passed from one mast or spar to the next.

How can you now set about making a wool picture of your own?

You will need a piece of fairly stiff but reasonably open-weave cloth, like needlework canvas or linen; wool which should be creamy-coloured for the sails, blue, green and grey for the sea and the sky, and black or brown for the hull. You will need other coloured scraps of wool for such things as decorations on the ship, pennants and flags. You will also need heavy thread or about a three-strand thickness of embroidery thread for the rigging, needles and a pair of scissors.

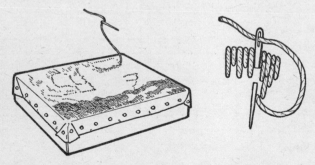

Ideally you should have a box frame on which to mount your canvas as you sew. You can make this from four lengths of flat wood joined at the corners. Spread the canvas tightly over it and fix the sides down with drawing pins. This box frame acts as a rather rough embroidery hoop, keeping the material stretched as you stitch.

Draw your ship on the canvas with a felt-tip pen. It may also be useful, if you are not copying from a picture of an original ship, to draw your ship on a piece of paper first so that you can refer to it as the canvas begins to be covered with stitches.

Work the background first using long and short stitch so that all the material is covered, except for the ship. Then work the ship itself in the space you have left. Use shorter stitches for the hull, longer ones for the sails. If you want to make the sails look as if they billow out, cut small pieces of thin foam rubber 2 mm ($\frac{1}{10}$ in) smaller all round than the size of the sail. Glue these on to your canvas and work over them, using stitches that reach from one side to the other of the sail.

Finish off the picture by sewing on the rigging using thick thread. This could be done in back stitch or chain stitch (see page 8), or you could use longer lines that you simply sew as a single stitch from one mast to the other as necessary.

You will, if you are satisfied with your work, probably want to frame your picture. You could get it done professionally, although it is rather expensive. You could buy a frame, either an old one or a ready-made one. You could mount your picture on a board or heavy card and fix down a heavy card frame or a wooden one around it. If you want to protect the picture, as a normal frame with glass would do, you could get a sheet of perspex to cover it.

It is worth investigating the prices of all these ways of framing this and other pictures, because the cost of materials is such that it may cost very little more to buy a ready-made frame than to make your own.

4 Using paper and paint

Papercutting

Victorian ladies had many pastimes. The Industrial Revolution
had brought a new wealth and a new leisure to the middle classes,
though to the workers it often brought an even harder and
gloomier life than the hardships suffered by the agricultural
peasants. But for the better-off it was a great period for a variety
of decorative occupations in the home: needlework of all kinds,
shellwork, painting and papercutting, including making
silhouettes. In Poland and Germany too papercutting has been an
active craft, often using traditional peasant designs. In countries
as far apart as Mexico and China colourful cut-paper work was
often linked with funerals or used as talismans to ward off the
'evil eye'.

You can start papercutting with no more than a pair of scissors
(for fine work you will need very pointed ones like embroidery
scissors) and some paper. The better assortment of gummed and
plain paper you have, the greater variety of work you can do. A
paper scalpel is a useful tool but be sure to learn how to change the
blade safely, and always remember how sharp the blade is! A good
paper glue, a ruler, a compass and a pencil are useful for some
work. A strong sheet of smooth cardboard is very useful as a work
surface and cutting board, especially when you are using your
scalpel.

There are a few simple rules about papercutting which it is best
to know about rather than learn from experience.

1 Cut the most complicated parts first so that the paper doesn't
flop about too much.

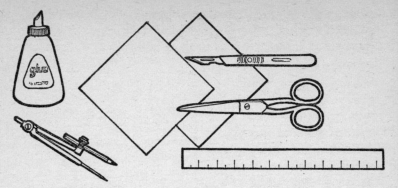

2 Cut the surplus paper away quite often so that it doesn't hang down, tangling with your scissors and tearing the pattern.

3 Cut right-hand bends from below and left-hand bends from above. This again will help you to avoid tearing and bending the paper.

4 When you are cutting out an area in the middle of the design, hold the paper down flat on your cutting board and make the first incision with your scalpel. Work outwards from this cut.

5 Make sure you don't cut through the points where the pattern holds together or bits will drop out when you don't want them to.

Snowflakes

This is one of the simplest forms of papercutting and one that you may well have tried before. Using your compass, draw a number of different sized circles on white paper. Snowflakes always have six points, so, using the compass again, divide the circle into six equal segments. (Follow the first three instructions for making the template for patchwork on page 15.)

Fold the circle in half, then fold each side piece over the centre. Fold gently so that the paper stays in position but doesn't crease excessively.

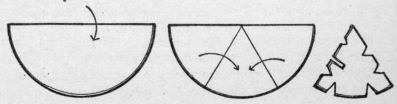

Now cut out patterns around the edge and along the folds, making sure you don't cut right along a fold. Open out the circle. To remove the creases, put the circle under a sheet of thin paper and press it with a warm iron.

When you have cut out several snowflakes in this way, mount them on a sheet of coloured paper with some of them slightly overlapping so they appear like snowflakes falling through the sky.

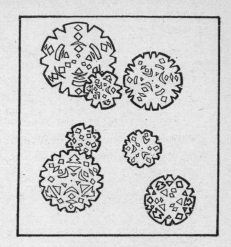

Other folded cut-outs

Try experimenting with more folds. For eight parts, fold the paper in half, in half again, and in half yet again. For sixteen sections, fold it yet again. Thirty-two sections (another fold needed!) is probably as many folds as most papers will take. Also try cutting more formal shapes so that you get a regular pattern.

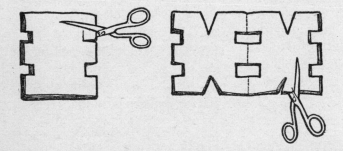

Make your cuts while the paper is folded in sixteen sections. Then open it out to eight sections and make another series of cuts. Note how the different cuts turn out when you open out the paper so that you can use them again in another design.

Symmetrical silhouettes

For symmetrical silhouettes you only fold the paper once. Draw your picture on one side of the paper. Start cutting from the edge and work towards the centre. This will help to keep the two layers together better than if you cut from the fold outwards. See how skilful you can become in cutting away more and more of the paper. Mount the finished silhouette on backing paper.

Mixing colour and shape

A great number of pictures can be built up using different layers of cut-out paper in a variety of colours.

Cutting within a frame

This sort of cut-work requires more skill as you are cutting a picture from a single sheet of paper. You will need to work out your design before you start cutting and draw it on the back of the paper. Take great care when you are planning the picture that bits are not going to be completely cut round so that they fall away. Start cutting from the inside and work outwards. If your picture is going to have a frame make sure that the design is still attached to it at least once on each side. Stick your picture carefully on to a backing card.

Stained glass pictures

You can make very pretty pictures with scraps of coloured tissue or cellophane fixed within the cut-out frame.

Making silhouettes

As with other papercutting the main equipment is paper, a pencil and scissors. For silhouette-making you also need a lamp, such as an adjustable desk lamp, and some drawing pins.

Fix a large sheet of drawing paper to a suitable wall with the drawing pins. (When we say 'suitable' we mean one your parents don't mind you putting drawing pins into!) Sit the person whose silhouette or likeness is to be taken on a chair close to the wall. Stand the light on the other side of the person, so it throws a distinct shadow of his or her profile on to the paper. Position your model so that the shadow is as near life-size as possible.

You can get your model really close in and steady if you put a tall glass, like a wine glass, between the model's head and the wall.

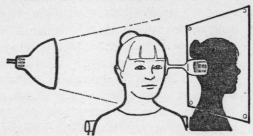

Now sketch the head and shoulders of your sitter on the paper. Do this carefully but swiftly because your model will only be able to sit absolutely still for a very brief period and any movement is bound to affect your drawing.

When you have completed the outline, and released your sitter, cut out the head using your scalpel along the line.

The centre part is put aside, leaving the outline. Lay this on a sheet of stiff black paper so that the head appears in black and fix it down carefully with glue, making sure that the glue doesn't squeeze out on to the head.

Kite making

Kites have been used throughout history in a number of surprisingly different ways. In 200 BC a Chinese general used a kite to calculate the distance between his troops and a castle they wanted to attack. He was then able to dig a tunnel under the castle walls and take the enemy by surprise. In eastern countries kites have had a religious significance for hundreds of years, and are thought to ward off evil spirits. The kites from China, Japan, Korea, Indonesia, Cambodia and Vietnam come in a multitude of shapes and sizes – birds, dragons, snakes and butterflies. For several months in the spring these spectacular kites are used in huge kite-flying festivals. In Thailand the competitors try to entangle each others kites, whilst in China and Korea the tails of the kites are covered with pieces of glass and the combatants try to slice through each other's lines.

Kites were not only useful in war and festivities: Benjamin Franklin helped to discover the modern lightning conductor by experimenting with a kite equipped with metal spikes. They have also been used to pull carriages and boats, and nowadays people even harness themselves to kites in the sport called hang-gliding. These kites, known as delta planes, can keep a man airborne for long periods. Without kites the modern aeroplane might never have been invented, for the Wright brothers began their experiments in flying with a simple kite glider. Kites are usually made from cloth or paper attached to a light wooden framework. They come in many different shapes and sizes, some have tails, others are tailless.

Making a fish kite

This comes from Japan. It represents a carp which symbolizes courage and endurance. Every year on the fifth day of the fifth month the Japanese celebrate Boy's Day, by flying a paper carp for every boy in the family.

To make the carp kite you will need two large sheets of green tissue paper, some smaller pieces in contrasting colours, a piece of wire long enough to form a circle to make the fish's mouth, and a ball of string.

Draw and cut the two main body shapes, (about ¾ metre or 30 in long) from the green tissue. Add some eyes and fins with the other colours (but don't use too much glue). You should cut all the tissue paper parts in pairs so that the kite is completely symmetrical.

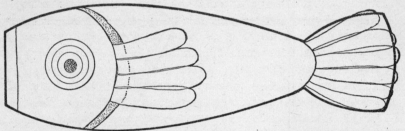

Glue the two body pieces together leaving the mouth and tail free so that the wind can blow through. Make a hoop with the piece of wire, securing the ends by twisting them round and round. Fit the hoop into the fish's mouth, folding the edges of the tissue paper over it. Either sellotape or glue the mouth carefully so as not to tear the tissue.

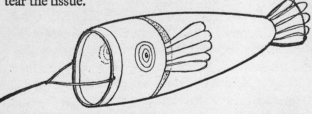

Fasten a piece of string on either side of the mouth and attach this to a longer line. The carp is now ready to fly upstream!

Making a diamond-shaped kite

The more conventional diamond-shaped kite is also easy to make. The frame consists of two pieces of light bamboo or dowel – a long piece for the lengthwise support and a shorter one to go across the kite. Find the exact centre of each piece and bind them together with a length of string or thin wire.

Cut the sail of the kite out of paper – newspaper, wrapping paper, or tissue are ideal. The sail should be 1 cm ($\frac{1}{2}$ in) larger than the frame and perfectly symmetrical. Glue one side of the frame and place it on the paper sail. Glue down 1 cm ($\frac{1}{2}$ in) all the way round the edge of the sail, taking in the frame.

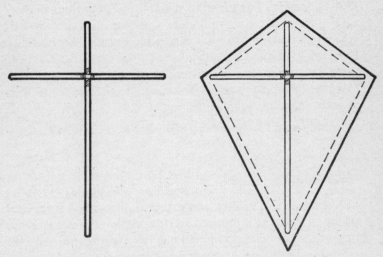

Make a tail by cutting strips of tissue or crêpe paper 2–3 cms ($1-1\frac{1}{4}$ in) wide. Twist the pieces round a length of string at 10-cm (4-in) intervals.

A dab of glue will help to secure the paper.

Attach the tail to the bottom of the kite with a small piece of sellotape. The tail will help to stabilize the kite, but if it is too heavy the kite will not take off.

Tape a piece of string to either end of the horizontal support – it should be about three times the distance between each point. Attach each free end to a curtain ring. The flying line is then attached to this ring and the kite is ready to fly. Your flying line will be easier to handle if you wind it round a length of broom handle or any smooth piece of wood. This will give you more to hold on to and thus more control than just holding a ball of string.

Find out which way the wind is blowing. Put the kite on the ground with the string underneath and the tail facing away from the wind. Now walk for ten metres into the wind unwinding the kite string. If there is plenty of wind a few short tugs on the kite string will be enough to get the kite off the ground. If there is not very much wind you should be able to get the kite off the ground by running into the wind.

Don't fly your kite near overhead wires and if ever in doubt, let go!

Marbling

The origins of marbling are shrouded in mystery. Most people think of Italy as the home of real marble, but nobody knows who discovered the method for making paper that resembled the cold and beautiful stone. Marbled paper has been used a great deal in the past for decorating the covers and endpapers of books. This is one way in which you might like to use your marbled paper. It is a fascinating craft, and requires very little skill or equipment! You will find it full of surprises as it is impossible to have complete control over the pattern you are making, and no two pieces of marbled paper are ever exactly the same.

You will need an old baking tray, about 30 cm (12 in) square and at least 2 cm (1 in) deep. This is to hold the water which has to be prepared by adding a special powder called size. You should be able to buy a packet of size in a hardware or craft shop. Prepare the size by mixing 50 g (2 oz) of the powder with $\frac{1}{2}$ litre (1 pint) of boiling water. Add another 1½ litres (3 pints) of hot water and stir until the size has thoroughly dissolved. Allow the mixture to get cold.

Have some clean yoghurt pots or jam jars ready. Put a little oil paint into each jar (a different colour in each one). Add a little paint thinner. You should add just enough so that the paint will drop from a paint brush held above the jar.

You will need some sort of tool to swirl the paint into a marbled design. A good marbling comb can be made very simply from a piece of thick cardboard. Cut V-shaped nicks in the card with a sharp knife. Another method is to stick or sellotape a row of pins on to a strip of paper and then sandwich them between two pieces of thick cardboard. If you had double-sided sellotape, you could use it to fix down the pins on one card and fix the cards together.

A knitting needle is also a useful tool for making patterns.

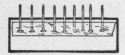

Cut several sheets of paper (most kinds of paper will do, but it should not have a glossy surface). The paper should be a little smaller than the baking tray, so that you can lift it out easily.

Fill the tray almost full with the size mixture and drop two or three drops of paint on the surface. If you want a multi-coloured design use different colours and swirl them together. You will find that by using different tools in a variety of ways (up and down, across, round in a circle) you will be able to produce an endless number of patterns. When you are satisfied with the design you can see on the surface, lay a piece of paper gently on the water. When you can see the design appearing faintly on the reverse side of the paper lift it out and allow it to dry. You can either lay your marbled paper on a wad of newspaper which will blot up the surplus water, or hang it on a makeshift clothes line – make sure there is something underneath to catch the drips! Before you begin another pattern you will have to clean the surface of the water. Fold a piece of newspaper several times (it should be the width of the tray), and draw the newspaper over the surface. This should blot up any paint still left.

You could use your marbled paper as a special writing paper. In this case you should use fairly pale-coloured paints, or you may find it difficult to see your writing! If the paper buckles up when it is drying you can iron it very carefully with a warm iron. You could also use the marbled paper for wrapping presents or, as we suggested earlier, for making endpapers for a book.

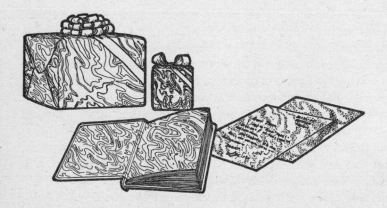

Paper beads

Here is another use for that versatile material paper. You can use newspaper or pages from magazines which have lightweight paper to make beads for unusual necklaces and bracelets.

Cut long strips of paper. The longer the strip the larger the bead. The width of each bead will be the same as the paper width. Taper some strips at one end. You will find as you work how different kinds of strips will make different kinds of beads.

Straight strips make plain cylindrical beads. You can make variations on this by adding a narrow strip on top of the wider first strip, or adding wider strips on top of a narrow first strip.

Tapered strips make up into oval-shaped beads and you can experiment with different widths of tapering and lengths of paper so that you can make long, slender oval beads or almost circular beads.

Wind the strips carefully round a knitting needle, gluing each layer of paper to the layer beneath. Remove the needle from the bead and put it aside so that the glue can dry thoroughly.

You can use the beads as they are, varnishing them with a light clear varnish or with clear nail varnish, or you can paint them either in plain colours or in patterns with enamel paint or coloured nail varnish.

For necklaces you thread the beads on to a length of cotton or nylon thread. Tie the ends together for a long necklace or fasten the ends on to a necklace clip (which you will be able to buy in a craft shop) if you want to make a short necklace.

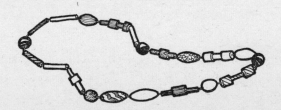

 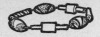

For bracelets you will need to use a fine elastic thread so that you can pass the bracelet over your hand.

These paper beads would also be very suitable in a bead curtain (see page 61) as they are very light.

Making rubbings

Brass rubbings have made very popular wall hangings since the early nineteenth century. Memorial brasses are set into the floors of many old churches. These are brass plaques engraved with the figure or coat of arms of a person who either lies buried in the church under the plaque, or who lived in the area but died far away.

The figures are of knights and their ladies, sometimes with their children and their pets. Memorial brasses date from the thirteenth century onwards and can be found in churches in Britain and northern Europe. There are about 8,000 in England, mainly in the south-east.

Brass rubbings are taken from these plaques, but you can take rubbings of almost anything which has an uneven surface, so whether or not you have memorial brasses in your local churches, you can learn how to make rubbings in preparation for the day when you find a real memorial brass.

The best materials for rubbing are a soft pencil, or better, a wax crayon, and some paper. You can make your first rubbing as soon as you have this equipment. If you have a coin handy, start now!

Cover the coin with the paper, hold the paper down firmly and rub across the surface of the coin with the side of the crayon. You have made a rubbing!

Experiment with other rubbings. Take rubbings from keys, carved wood, paper clips, a piece of lace, anything which is flattish and has an interesting texture.

Leaf rubbings

Try making leaf rubbings. Fix the leaves on a bit of smooth card with a dab of glue, cover with paper and rub gently across the leaf with a wax crayon, always working in the same direction. It will be difficult to keep within the edges of the leaf all the time, so you may like to cut out the rubbings and mount them on a backing sheet. Use different coloured crayons, making some leaves green, others fading through the browns, oranges, reds and yellows of autumn colours.

You could use your leaf rubbings to make cards, pictures, calendars and bookmarks, or you could make a collection of different leaves just as you would make a collection of pressed, dried leaves.

Bark rubbings

You could add bark rubbings to a collection of leaf rubbings.
Take a sheet of paper and your crayons. Fix the paper on to the
tree with sellotape. Make the rubbing with the side of the crayon.
If you are making a collection, always be sure that you know the
name of the tree so you can write captions for your collection on
each page.

Coal-hole and manhole covers

In some city streets where the nineteenth century houses were
built with coal cellars which stretched out under the pavement,
the coal man used to pour the coal directly into the cellar through
a coal-hole. These holes were often covered over with very
decorative covers set into the pavement.

You can make lovely rubbings from these covers. Clean air zones
and central heating have reduced the number of people who have
these coal-holes and they have often been removed and the holes
paved over. However you may be lucky enough to still have some
in your neighbourhood.

Rubbings of these coal-hole covers are now becoming collectors'
pieces, so at this point we explain how the 'professional' goes
about making a rubbing, and tell you about the materials you will
need for this craft.

Equipment and materials

Heelball or brass rubbing crayons Heelball is a mixture of wax and
lampblack which is used by cobblers and is the original material
that brass rubbers used. You may be able to buy some from your
local shoe repairers if you explain what you need it for. There
are, however, special brass rubbing sticks or blocks on the
market (called Astral Heelball) which you could buy at a craft
shop. (Phillips and Page Ltd, of 50 Kensington Church St,
London W8, are the brass rubbing specialists. If you live outside
London, you can order their materials from Phillips and Page Ltd,
40 Elm Hill, Norwich, Norfolk.) You can carry on with your wax
crayons, but get the wide, stubby ones which cover a greater area
and are less pointed.

Paper Rolls of lining paper can be bought from decorator's shops quite reasonably. If you decide to make rubbings on coloured paper, remember that it must not be too stiff or thick or shiny. For special rubbings you can use architect's detail paper. This does not yellow with age, but like all good papers is quite expensive. There are specially recommended brass rubbing papers which you can order from Phillips and Page Ltd.

Masking tape This is a special sort of adhesive tape which will hold down but not tear the paper and will not mark the things it is stuck to. When you take to rubbing memorial brasses, you may find that the church insists on you using masking tape as it cannot damage the surface of the brass.

Scissors

A *small soft brush* This is very useful to clean off grit and dirt on a coal-hole cover or on a brass plaque.

A *clean cloth* This is to wipe the cover or the brass extra clean and to wipe your hands and the paper to keep them clean whilst you work.

How to make the coal-hole rubbing

First clean off the coal-hole cover very carefully. Any bits of grit left either on the surface or in the pattern indentations will show on your rubbing. Finish off with your cloth to get rid of the bits you can't even see.

Fix your paper down over the cover with the masking tape. Rub over the entire cover with the cloth, so that you can see the edge of the cover on the paper and can keep within this line while you work.

Rub all over the cover evenly with the heelball, rubbing firmly and covering every part. When the whole cover pattern has been transferred to your paper, wipe off any loose bits of crayon or heelball with the clean cloth and polish off the rubbing with the cloth to give it an extra gloss.

Brass rubbing

When you come to a real church brass you follow the instructions we have given already. There are, however, a few important extra instructions. You *must* ask permission to take a brass rubbing from the vicar of the church. It is often wise to ask in advance to make sure that no one has 'booked up' ahead of you. You will normally be asked to pay a small fee which goes towards the upkeep of the church. Many churches do not allow brass rubbing on Sundays, for obvious reasons.

Many memorial brasses are now protected from the wear of passing feet by carpets. Take off your shoes while you are working so that *you* don't scratch or damage the surface. When you have completed your work, clean up carefully and cover the brass over just as you found it.

Remember to note down the name of the church, the name of the person to whom the plaque was dedicated and its date. There will often be a card giving this information posted up in the church.

Not all churches have brasses and if you want to find out where to go rubbing, many of the books listed in the book list section tell you where to find different kinds of brasses. Phillips and Page Ltd also sell duplicated pamphlets listing the brasses in various parts of the country.

Some variations on rubbings

Try using coloured wax crayons or heelball to make a rubbing in one all-over colour, or colour different parts of the brass rubbing in different colours. You might, for instance, use one colour for the armour and others for the features, details of dress and any accompanying pet.

Try using black paper with white crayon or coloured paper with black or another darkish colour.

Try making rubbings of inscriptions, either on brass plaques or on old tombstones in the churchyard.

Mounting your rubbings

As we have already suggested, you can use small rubbings to decorate cards and calendars. You could make a wall picture with

coal-hole cover rubbings mounted on light card and fix it up on your wall with a material like Blutack.

You will need to mount full length brass rubbings so that they lie flat against the wall. You can buy poster holders which have a hanger rail at the top and a second rail at the bottom to weigh down the picture, and a cord for hanging. The more traditional hangers are made from wooden rods and cord. You will need two lengths of narrow rod slightly wider than your paper and a length of cord or good string. Roll the ends of the paper twice round each rod, fixing them with glue. Tie or nail the cord at either end of the top rod.

5 Using all sorts of materials

Leatherwork

It was probably about two million years ago that man first discovered a primitive form of clothing. However, his wardrobe was very different from ours! All his clothes were made from animal skins and furs. Nowadays leather coats, skirts, bags and belts are very expensive and people often make do with imitation leather and furs. But nothing can equal the feel and smell of real leather. Eskimos in the cold polar lands wear leather and fur for warmth, South American Gauchos use it for its hard-wearing qualities, and North American Indians make colourful and exciting traditional clothes by beading and fringing the leather.

With a few basic tools, some leather, and a little practice you will be able to make your own leather clothes and accessories for a fraction of the price they would be in the shops. You can glue leather, stitch it, paint on it, and cut it without fear of it fraying, and whatever you make will probably last a lifetime!

What you need for leatherwork

A *good working surface*, like a piece of smooth hardboard.

A steel *ruler*.

A sharp *scalpel* with some spare blades.

A leather plier-type *hole punch* with different-sized heads.

A *skiving knife* (which has a short blade with a wide bevelled end).

A *hammer* (it is better to have a special leatherwork or wooden hammer).

An *awl* (for making holes).

A *stitch marker*.

Glovers needles (very strong with a triangular-shaped point).
Strong *glue* (Copydex is a good all-purpose glue).

Buying leather

It is not usually too difficult to buy leather. You can either buy a whole skin, or in some cases you can buy bags of off-cuts from craft shops which are suitable for making belts, purses, and small bags. If you are buying a whole skin examine it carefully for any blemishes or thin patches which could spoil your finished product. There are several different kinds and quality of leather available and the following are among the most commonly used:

Hide This is a tough, heavy leather that we get from cows. It is used for making shoes, bags, and heavy belts.

Calf This is a softer leather which is good for tooling. It is more expensive than hide but nice to work with.

Pigskin A fine soft leather which you will recognize by the fine holes in the surface. It is usually very expensive.

Suede This can be any leather which is given a special finish on the wrong side giving it a velvety feel.

Morocco This is goatskin and can be used for making practically anything. It is very popular for bookbinding.

Snakeskin These skins are often paper-thin, and therefore need careful handling. They make good belts when given a stronger backing.

Before you begin to make a finished piece of leatherwork it would be a good idea to experiment with some off-cuts.

Joining leather

If you are using one of the finer skins such as calf or pigskin you can sew the pieces together on an ordinary machine, gluing the seams open afterwards. Most skins however are too tough to push a needle through and this is where an awl and hammer come in handy! First decide where you want the line of stitching. Mark a straight line with a stitch marker, and then make holes for the stitches by hammering the awl into the leather.

Skiving

This is a process by which thin layers of leather are shaved away to reduce the thickness where several pieces are to be glued together. It is quite difficult and needs practice. Place the skin face down on a smooth cutting surface. Hold the skiving knife almost flat and very carefully shave away a thin layer of leather where the join is to be. Be very careful as the knife is very sharp, so always skive away from your body. Repeat this on both pieces and you will find that after you have glued them together you will have a nice smooth seam.

Thonging

A very easy and effective way of joining two pieces of leather is by a lacing process. A thong is a long thin strip of leather. Cut out a circle of leather with a diameter of 15 cm (6 in). Starting from the outside cut a thin even strip, about 3 mm ($\frac{1}{8}$ in) wide.

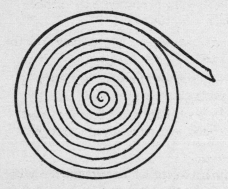

Carefully measure and mark on your leather where you want the holes for the thonging to go. Make sure that these holes are exactly opposite each other. With the plier-type hole punch make the holes in the leather (the holes should be the same size as the thong). Paper clips are useful for holding two pieces of leather together whilst you are threading the thong through. Taper one end of the thong so that you can thread it through a large-eyed needle. Start the thonging by gluing the end to the wrong side of your work. Thread the thong through the holes using one of the methods shown here.

Make sure that the thonging does not get twisted, and that the right side stays uppermost.

Decorating your leather

You can paint designs straight on to the surface of leather using either an oil-based paint or one of the shoe dyes you can buy in shoe shops. However, if you want to colour your leather smoothly all over you will have to stain the surface using a special stain powder which is mixed to a paste with methylated spirit. This is applied gently with cotton wool using a circular movement. The faster you can work the smoother the result will be.

Tooling

This is the method used for making a design on leather. Certain areas are stamped or gouged with special or makeshift tools, leaving other areas raised. Work out your design on a piece of paper and transfer it to the right side of the leather. Dampen the surface of the leather. This makes the leather soft so that you can 'tool' it. When it dries the pattern will harden. You can buy special tools for making patterns but they are also quite easy to make. You can use anything that can be hammered into the leather to make a clear impression. Screw heads are very effective and can be attached to a piece of dowel to make it easier to hammer them on to the leather. When you have finished your design and the leather has thoroughly dried you can stain the raised surfaces to make the design stand out even more.

Appliqué

Because leather does not fray it is a perfect material to use for appliqué work. Simply cut out shapes from scraps of suede or soft leather and glue them to the piece you want to decorate.

You could cut the shapes out with pinking shears to give them a zigzag edge.

Beading

North American Indians are the experts at using beads and leather, but you can copy their methods. Thread a fine needle with strong thread and make a knot at the end. Bring the needle to the surface of the leather and thread on four beads. Pass the needle back through to the wrong side and up again just after the second bead. Put the needle through the third and fourth bead and pick up four new beads. Continue this method along the line of your design.

You can also thread beads on to thin strips of leather, or a fringe of leather to make decorative thonging or edgings. Knot the ends so that the beads don't drop off!

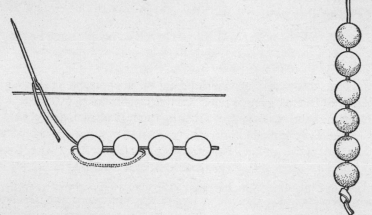

Making a tooled belt

When you are making a particular leather object or garment it is important to work out an accurate pattern beforehand. Thin card is particularly good as you can lay it flat on the leather and trace round it.

To make a belt, cut a pattern for a long strip 30 cm (12 in) longer than your waist measurement, and about 5 cm (2 in) wide with a shaped point at one end. Place the pattern on your leather (a thick cow hide would be suitable) and draw round it. Mark a

point 5 cm (2 in) from the unshaped end in the centre of the belt
and punch a hole for the prong of the buckle to go through. With
the skiving knife pare down this end to reduce the thickness when
it is glued back.

Dampen the surface of the leather and tool your chosen design
on the belt. You could either make the design just round the edge
of the belt or all over! If the surface gets dry whilst you are still
working, damp it down again. When you have finished tooling
allow the belt to dry thoroughly. You can now stain the surface
and edges of the belt using the method previously described.
Attach the buckle to the unshaped end of the belt pushing the
prong through the hole you punched. Fold back the pared down
turning and glue this to the wrong side of the belt. Measure where
you want the holes in your belt and using the correct size of hole,
punch four or five holes spaced at regular intervals.

Making clay pots

Long before the potter's wheel was invented people were making
clay pots. In many places they still make pots without a wheel.
When we lived in West Africa, every market day women used to
pass our house carrying loads of great black pots which they had
made and were taking to sell. Every pot was alike and yet every
pot was slightly different, expressing the skill of each potter and
her mood as she made it.

So not having a wheel is not a particular problem to a potter. A
more real problem is how to 'fire' your pots, that is how to bake
them in a heat hot enough to make the clay melt and fuse together
so that the pots become strong and lasting. To make the pots
waterproof you need to glaze them and fire them again. To fire or
glaze pottery you really need a kiln, and kilns are expensive.

It is possible, if you live in the country and have your parents'
permission, to experiment with the most primitive form of firing,
laying the pots on a base of stones and firebricks and baking them
in the centre of a bonfire. But you will not be able to reach the heat
required for glazing in this way. Ask advice about this. Often a
local potter is prepared to allow other potters to use space in his or
her kiln; sometimes the education authority or a school will have a
kiln where they will let you fire your pots.

We are not going to talk here about firing and glazing pottery. This, we feel, you must learn from the person who is going to give you access to a kiln.

Preparing the clay

You can buy the clay from some craft shops and potteries. Ask for a coarse rather than a fine clay as it is easier to work with.

Mix the clay with enough water to make it into a stiff paste. Leave it in the bowl you mixed it in for a few days. The clay needs to be dry enough to be picked up and laid out on a board. You may need to pour off some of the water if you have made it rather too wet. The clay will be ready to work when you can stick your finger into it and it comes out clean.

If you can't work with it straight away when it is ready, you can store it for a few days by covering it with a damp cloth or old towel in a cool place, or keeping it in a plastic bag or bin with a lid.

Clay has small bubbles in it which will burst when the pot is fired and cause weaknesses. To get rid of these you 'wedge' the clay. This is a process of cutting up the clay and pounding it together again. You can cut clay with an old knife, but professional potters use a cutting wire like a cheese wire. For small quantities a cheese wire bought at a kitchen shop would be quite suitable. For larger quantities you will want a real clay wire from a craft shop. Cut the lump in half and slam one piece down on the other, pushing the lumps back together. Do this several times to remove all the air bubbles. Now cut off a lump the size you want and knead it on the board like bread dough.

We describe here three methods of making pots for which no wheel is needed.

Making pinch pots

Take a lump of prepared clay which will fit your hand. Roll it into a ball. Hold it in one hand and with the thumb of your other hand make a hole about two thirds of the way through the ball.

Now, using your thumb inside the ball and your forefinger outside it, pinch the clay, turn the ball, pinch again and turn. Continue like this, turning and pinching, so that the sides of the pot grow taller and thinner all the time. You will learn how to shape the pot as you work with the clay. Smooth the top off to give the pot a good edge.

If you have no kiln, leave the pot to dry in a cool place for about two weeks, turning it from time to time. Your pots will not be waterproof, so if you want to use them for plants or flowers, you will need to put a small glass jar inside to hold the water.

Making coil pots

You make the coils, long 'sausages' of clay, by rolling the prepared clay on the board with your hands. They should be about 1.5 cm ($\frac{5}{8}$ in) in diameter. Coil them around on the board to make the base, pressing the coils together as you work.

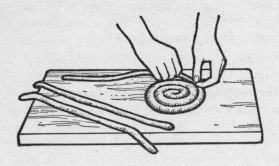

When the base is large enough, smooth the coils together on both sides, bending the edges upwards to make the beginning of the sides. Now build up the sides of the pot with more coils. As you use each coil, smooth it over inside and out. If you want the pot to go straight up, like a mug, put the coils directly on top of each other. If you want the pot to slope outwards, like a flowerpot, put the coils on with a slightly widening circumference. If you want the top of the pot to slope inwards, put on the coils with a slightly narrowing circumference.

Smooth the pot over inside and out and finish off the top edge. Some potters leave the outer coils, or rings of them, unsmoothed to give a rough decorative effect. You can make square, oval or oblong pots using the coil method, working from a base of one of these shapes.

Making slab pots

Slab pots are made by rolling out clay rather like pastry on the
board. Work between two strips of wood to keep the thickness of
the sheet of clay regular.

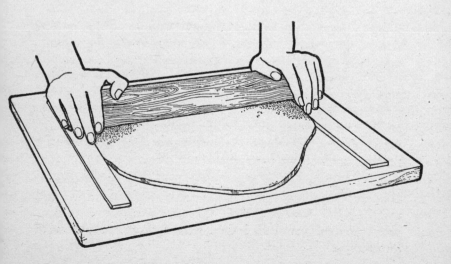

With an old knife and a ruler cut out a base and sides. Fix them
together with 'slip' (wet clay) and pressure from your fingers.

Handles, spouts and lids

If you want to make a jug, you need to make a lip or a spout.
To make a lip, put your index finger inside the pot and draw the
edge outwards, at the same time use your thumb and middle
finger to push outwards and upwards from the outside.

To make a spout, cut a circle in the side of your pot, on the
shoulder, and coil a spout around the hole, smoothing and pressing
the coils to the pot.

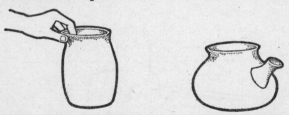

Shape a piece of clay in a roll to make the handle and fasten it to
the pot with slip. Make sure that the handle is large enough so that
you can get at least two fingers into it to hold the pot. The handle
will dry out faster than the main pot and this may cause it to split.
To avoid this, wrap the handle in a damp cloth or in a plastic bag
while the pot is drying. Take the cloth off half-way through the
process of drying.

Lids can be made either by the coil or the slab method. Make the
lid slightly larger than the top of the pot so that it won't slip

inside. Fix a strip of clay in a circle under the lid, the size of the inside of the pot, and it will hold the lid in position better. A ball of clay can be fixed on with slip for the knob.

Decorations

While the clay is still damp you can decorate your pots with indented marks and lines, with other coloured clays (the Engobe technique) and with glazes. You can buy special clay modelling tools to mark and decorate pottery, but you can use any smooth stick, the end of a teaspoon or a fork, to make the decorations. Engobe decorations are put on while the original clay is still damp. You can buy Engobe and prepare it as instructed and paint it on to the pot. You can also buy metal-oxides with which to colour white clay to make your own Engobe. We will not go into the matter of glazing here as you do need a kiln for it, and once you have reached the stage where you need access to a kiln you will need to do some further reading and research in the craft of potting. We list on page 137 a few books which might be useful to you.

Mexican dough art

This is an ancient folk-craft which is cheap, easy and fun to do. You will probably find all the things you need in your kitchen, but don't forget to ask before you use them!

The origins of the craft are wrapped up in the history of bread-making, which dates back many thousands of years. Bread was a symbol of wealth and prosperity to the Egyptians, but it was the Greeks who first began to use bread dough in a decorative way. Since these early beginnings bakers all over the world have continued to perfect the craft – you can see examples of their work at the time of the Harvest Festival, when huge loaves shaped like wheat-sheafs are used to decorate churches.

However, not all dough is edible! The dough figures and ornaments that Mexico is famous for are rock hard and brilliantly coloured, with a shiny varnished outer coating. In Equador they use dough to make frames for mirrors and pictures, but with a little practice and experience you can make practically anything from dough.

There are different ways of making inedible modelling dough, and we give recipes for two of them. Apart from the ingredients for the dough itself you will need some modelling tools, paints, a paint brush, varnish, aluminium foil, and a baking sheet. The modelling tools can be very simple – a small kitchen knife, knitting needle, fork, sieve and biscuit cutter could all come in handy! If you want to make a hanging ornament or a dough flower with a stem, you will also need some thin wire.

Recipe 1
150 g (6 oz) flour
75 g (3 oz) salt
227 ml (8 fluid oz) warm water

Mix the flour and salt together in a large mixing bowl, and using a wooden spoon or your hands, gradually mix in the water. When the mixture has come together, turn it on to a lightly floured surface and start kneading! This means using your knuckles and working hard to get the dough into a manageable state. If the dough seems too sticky add some more flour, but if it is dry and crumbly you may need a little more water. When the dough is smooth and pliable put it into a plastic bag, and use as much as you need at a time. The dough does not keep well, so you should start modelling as soon as possible.

You can colour the dough at this stage by taking a piece of the dough, dabbing some paint or vegetable dye on it (you will only need a tiny amount) and kneading it again to mix the colour in. You may however, decide to leave the dough its natural colour – it will be a warm brown colour after baking. The other alternative is to paint your model after it has been baked. The baking time depends on the shape and size of your article. It is better when you are first experimenting to make small shapes, as the larger, more solid shapes sometimes warp in the oven. The oven should be set at 180°C (350°F, gas mark 4), and the dough should be ready in about half an hour. If you decide to leave the dough in its natural state you should glaze it with milk or egg yolk before baking. This will give the object a shiny, rich brown colour.

As an experiment to start with, try making a series of different-shaped pendants. Roll out the dough so that it is about the same thickness as a coin. Using a knife or pastry cutters make different shapes. If you want to hang the pendants after they have been baked, make holes in them at this point. You can also make a loop from a piece of wire and push this into the dough before baking.

You could make dough beads with the left-over scraps by rolling small pieces between your hands, making round balls, and sticking a knitting needle through them to make a hole for threading.

When the pendants are ready put them on to a piece of aluminium foil, place this on a baking sheet and put in the oven. When they are baked and quite cool you can paint them – ordinary water-colour paints or felt-tip pens are ideal. They should then be varnished for added protection. One of the easiest ways to do this is with an aerosol spray varnish. Although your finished object will seem very hard it is also very fragile, and will break like china if you drop it.

Recipe 2

3 pieces of white bread without crusts
1 tablespoon of white glue
2 teaspoons of glycerine

Tear the bread into small pieces and mix with the glue in a mixing bowl. When the dough is beginning to come together, add the glycerine and knead well. You can use this dough in exactly the same way as the dough previously described.

Try rolling the dough out using a rolling pin, and cut it into long, straight strips, about 1 cm ($\frac{1}{4}$ in) wide. Take three of these strips and plait them together. You could also make a rounded plait by rolling the strips into long 'sausages' before plaiting. You can use the plaits to make frames,

or if you form the plait into a circle you could make a mat.

The traditional Mexican dough figures are also fun to make. You could make a complete family together with animals! At Christmas time you could use your dough to make a Nativity set.

If you press your dough through a wide-meshed sieve or the hole of a colander you will get very thin strands which make ideal hair for your figures, or the prickles for a hedgehog! You can also use tools to make impressions in the dough.

The best way to enjoy the craft is to experiment, but don't forget to ask if it is all right for you to use the oven and kitchen equipment.

Candlemaking

After the light of the sun and the moon and the blaze of a fire, candles were man's first form of light and, for hundreds of centuries, almost his only form of artificial light. Early candles were a wick set in oil rather than in the firm wax we use to fuel our candles today.

This sort of oil light is still used by some people in poor countries today. In India at the festival of Diwali, little oil lights like these are put out on every window-sill and doorway. As children living in India we used to be taken out after dusk to see the town lit by these shimmering little lamps like thousands of stars come down to earth.

In Europe right up to a century ago poor people still used rush lights, which were made from the central pith of rushes dipped in oil. But rich people had candles made from beeswax or, more commonly, tallow candles made from hard animal fat. And rich people, of course, had gas lighting and electricity when they were invented. Through the centuries people have experimented with candles, trying to get the best light and the most beautiful effects with colour and shape. Now that candlemaking has come into its own again as a home craft, you will be able to borrow books at your library and get a great number of ideas from other candlemakers. Here we set out a few basic ideas so that you can begin.

A word of warning

Before you start there are a few important points to remember:

Wax is inflammable
Never leave a pan of wax on the stove unattended
Be very careful with hot wax
Always ask a grown-up to supervise you

If you ever spill hot wax on yourself (and spilling the occasional drip is almost inevitable), soak the spot in cold water immediately and only then take off the hot wax.

There are two main ways of making candles – moulding and dipping. Here we show you only the simpler process of moulding.

Equipment and materials

You will need the following household equipment:

A small *saucepan*, preferably with a pouring lip.

A *sugar thermometer* (you may have to buy this, but you can also use it for jam and sweet-making).

A metal *spoon* (for stirring).

Candle moulds (straight-sided tins, glazed pottery, glasses, bottles, cardboard moulds. Do not use plastic containers as the heat of the wax will melt the plastic).

A metal *knitting needle* or *skewer* (from which to suspend the wick in the wax).

A metal *washer* or *weight* (to hold the wick down straight in the wax).

Other materials needed will have to be got from a craft shop.

Paraffin wax This usually comes in large white blocks.

Stearin This material usually comes in a flaky form. It helps to make the candles more opaque – less transparent – and also helps to stop the wick smoking. You should use at least 10% of Stearin to wax and the more you use, up to one third, the better your candles are likely to be. Some suppliers have wax which is already mixed with Stearin for candlemaking. For this and other materials follow the instructions supplied where they conflict with what we say here, as it may suit that particular mixture best.

Wicks These are made of plaited cotton and treated so they will burn at the same rate as the wax.

Oil-based dyes Get these especially prepared for candlemaking if you can as they will have the correct colour density.

Vaseline This is useful to grease the mould with before you pour the wax in, and makes sure that the candle comes out easily.

Basic candle moulding

1 Tie one end of the wick (which should be about 5 cm (2 in) longer than the depth of the mould) through the metal washer or weight. Tie the other end to the centre of the skewer or knitting needle.

2 Break the wax into small pieces in the saucepan. (You will have to experiment to determine the correct amount you will need for each size of mould.)

3 Heat the wax gently on the stove.

4 Add the dye and stir it in as the wax melts.

5 When all the wax has melted and the dye dissolved and mixed, set the pan aside to cool a little. Smear the inside of the mould with vaseline.

6 Hang the skewer across the top of your mould so that the wick hangs down in the centre.

7 Pour the wax into the mould. The best heat is 82°C (180°F). If the wax is smoking it is too hot. If the wax has become too cool, heat it up again.

8 Leave the wax to cool and become solid. When it has hardened it will contract away from the side of the mould and you will be able to pull the candle out.

9 Trim the wick to about 1 cm ($\frac{1}{2}$ in) above the wax.

Striped candles

You will need a choice of dyes, depending on how many different coloured stripes you want to make. You can of course use white as one colour and for those stripes you will need no dye.

Perhaps you could make a striped candle in the colours of the football team your family supports. My family supports Everton, so we would only need blue and white stripes. You could make a patriotic candle in red, white and blue or a Christmas Day candle in red and green with white.

You will need a mould, like a tin can. Make sure that there is no ridge on the inside of your mould which will stop the candle coming out. You will need wax, Stearin, a wick, two or more dye colours, and your usual candlemaking equipment including two saucepans.

1 Suspend the wick in the mould.

2 Put half the wax in each saucepan. You will need more pans for multi-coloured candles, of course. Add a different dye to each pan. If you want white stripes, leave one pan without dye.

3 Melt the wax in the pan with the colour you want for the first stripe until all the dye has been dissolved. Allow it to cool to the correct temperature. Pour this first colour into your mould to the depth you want your stripe.

4 Allow the first stripe to cool as you melt the second colour of wax. If you put in the second colour too soon it will blend into the first colour. (You might like to experiment with this on purpose another time.) Judging the moment correctly is one of the points at which practice will make perfect in your candlemaking attempts.

5 Pour in the wax for the second stripe.

6 Melt and heat the colours of wax alternately and pour further stripes.

7 Let the candle cool off, take it out of the mould and trim the wick.

You can aim to make equal depth stripes or irregular stripes so your candle may look like this:

By tipping the mould on a firm support as you fill it you can make slanting stripes going in different directions.

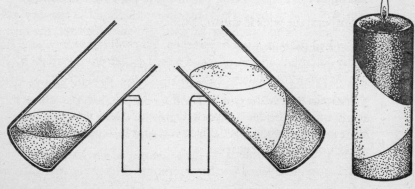

Make sure that the mould is fixed firmly on the slant so that it doesn't tip over and pour hot wax all over you!

A candle in a glass

If you have a pretty glass which you do not use regularly and which is not too delicate to take the hot wax, you can make a candle in it and use the glass as the candlestick.

An Advent candle

In Scandinavia many families burn an Advent candle each night in December up until Christmas Eve to mark the coming (the advent) of the Christ child.

You will need a very long thin mould to make one of these candles. A suitable mould be a long, cardboard cylinder of the sort used for storing posters and posting big sheets of paper and documents. You will need to make a base for the mould. Some of these cylinders have a plastic end which can be used. If yours does not, then use a cork or a plasticine plug.

You will need to make a candle with twenty-four stripes, so that one section can be burnt every night and the last one burnt on Christmas Eve. Make this last section deeper than the others so it will burn longer and also stand steadily. Make sure that your wick is long enough to go right down into this final section.

Make your Advent candle in the same way as you make other striped candles. When you have removed it from the mould, you could print the date on each stripe with adhesive letters like those made by Letraset.

Bottle-shaped candles

You can use an attractive shaped bottle as a mould, but you will have to break the bottle to extract your candle. You may find it easier to fill the bottle with wax if you use a funnel. Leave your bottle overnight to let the wax solidify right through.

When you want to remove the candle, put the bottle into a large, strong plastic bag. Place it on a sheet of newspaper on a hard surface. Carefully shatter the bottle with a hammer. Extract the glass very carefully, keeping it on the newspaper. Wrap the pieces of glass in the newspaper, put the parcel in the plastic bag and straight into the dustbin.

Scented candles

If you add an oil-based perfume to your candles, they will smell sweetly as they burn. You can add the fragrance by dipping the wick into the perfume before you make the candle. You will need to experiment to get the desired strength of scent. You may need to add a few drops of the scent to the wax with the dye to get it strong enough.

Some of the oil-based scents which you should be able to buy at a chemist are: oil of cloves for a spicy scent, pine for a Christmas candle, and sandalwood or violets for pretty summery smells. Store your scented candles in plastic bags or in an airtight box (like a freezer box) so that the scent does not evaporate.

Ships in bottles

In the days before high-speed, modern ships, sailors might spend weeks or months at sea without going ashore, and years at sea without going home. There was little to do on board, but the boredom itself and the men's creative energy urged them on to whittle and tie and sew and carve and plait. There were few materials to hand, but those that there were they exploited to the full – rope, string and thread, small pieces of wood and bone, and for the beautiful ships in bottles, the bottles in which their drink came. Many of the things that the sailors made were closely related to their life at sea – model ships, embroidered pictures of ships, and carvings of ships in whalebone. You can see exquisite examples of some of these creations at the National Maritime Museum in Greenwich (London), and the Glasgow Art Gallery, as well as in other museums in various places which are devoted to the sea.

How a ship in a bottle was made

The skill of making a full-rigged sailing ship which can slip through the neck of a bottle and ride there in full sail on its tiny sea was developed during the nineteenth century. The secret of this amazing phenomenon is that the ship is made outside the bottle with masts that fold down, and cross spars that can be turned at right angles to lie parallel with the length of the hull. The tiny ship is then inserted gently through the neck of the bottle and the masts are pulled upright by extensions of the rigging which run through the neck of the bottle. The sails are positioned with the help of a long pointer which is carefully manoeuvred through the neck.

Making these models requires enormous skill, patience, care, and good nimble fingers. We are not going to explain this craft further here (we recommend a full length book in the book list at the end of this book which explains all the details), but we can tell you how to make models in bottles which are not quite the real thing, but are very picturesque substitutes.

Ship in a jar

This sort of ship model can look highly professional, but it doesn't raise the fascinated questioning about how the ship got into the bottle.

You need an ordinary clear jar, like a jam jar, with a wide neck; balsa wood for the hull; cocktail sticks or toothpicks for the masts; dark thread for the rigging, stiff paper for the sails and a good, clear glue.

Carve the hull of your ship in balsa wood. Paint it and let it dry thoroughly. Use the cocktail sticks or toothpicks to make the masts. Make each mast separately and then fix it in the hull, making small holes in the wood and gluing the mast in place.

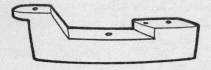

Make small cuts in the masts to take the horizontal cross spars. Glue the spars in position. When the glue is dry, put on a small dab of glue and bind the join with thread for extra strength. (Make sure that the height of the mast and the width of the cross spars will not stop the boat going into the neck of the bottle!)

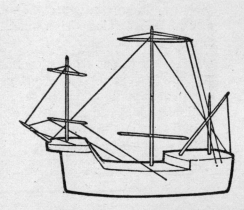

Make the rigging when the masts are fixed firmly to the hull.

The thread for the rigging can be tied or glued to the masts. If you want the sails to 'billow' out in the wind, roll each bit of sail round a pencil before you fix it on. Flags and pennants can be made with coloured papers and you can decorate the sails as you wish.

Before you put your finished boat into the jar, you need to make the 'sea' for it to sail on. Use melted candle wax dyed bluey-green by mixing it with poster paints or candlemaking dye. Spoon the melted wax into the jar very carefully. The wax will be very hot and you don't want it to splash up the side of the jar if you can avoid it. While the wax is beginning to set, flick the surface into 'waves' with a fork or stick. When the wax is fully set paint 'white horses' on the sea with a long-handled brush and white paint. Make a furrow in the wax with a skewer heated in a candle or

gas flame. (Hold the skewer with a cloth because it will get hot along its full length!) Slip the ship's hull into this furrow so that it stands firmly when the wax hardens again. Screw the lid on the jar and your ship is complete.

Quill-masted ships

When our brother was little he invented a method of making simple ships which would go into bottles. He used goose quills for the masts. These quills were sufficiently flexible to bend back as the ship passed through the neck of the bottle and then spring back into position again. The real problem with this method is that you do need to have access to poultry so that you can get the feathers to use for the quills. Even when you use quills the cross spars can be no wider than the neck of the bottle, but the masts can be taller.

You can make a slightly different kind of ship in a jar by setting your fully rigged ship in its sea inside the lid of the jar (leaving a narrow furrow around the edge of the inside of the lid) and then screwing the jar on to the lid.

6 Using nature's harvest

Herbs, flowers and pot-pourri

Since earliest times people have used the leaves, roots and
flowers of the field and hedgerow to feed themselves, to cure
diseases and to beautify both their homes and themselves.

Here are a few ideas from these ancient arts which you might like
to try.

Drying your own herbs

Herbs are at their best fresh from the garden in summer. But in
winter it is good to have your own herbs dried, and they make very
welcome presents. You can buy little spice jars to store your herbs,
or you can save the bottles herbs and spices have been bought in
and re-label them with their new contents.

Here is a list of a good selection of herbs to grow and dry: mint,
tarragon, basil, chives, rosemary, sage, thyme and parsley. The
time they take to dry will vary.

Pick the herbs' leaves when the plants are growing well. Cut
sprigs with sharp scissors. Lay the herbs out (never mixing the
varieties) in single layers on paper on trays in the airing cupboard.
Try not to handle the leaves too much, but turn them over gently
two or three times a day so that they dry evenly. Never dry herbs
or other plants in the direct sunlight or they will lose their colour,
scent and fragrancy.

When the herbs are dry and almost brittle (which may take a
couple of weeks) take the dried leaves off the stalks. Crumble them
slightly and store them in your jars.

Lavender bags

Cut the sprigs of lavender from the plants, stems and all. Put them in an old pillowcase in the airing cupboard to dry. Leave them for about two or three weeks until you can strip the flowers off the stalks easily.

Make little bags from a fine cloth like muslin or lawn or fine taffeta. Decorate them with lace and ribbons, and fill them with the dried lavender flowers.

Pot-pourri

This is a mixture of fragrant flowers, aromatic or spicy-smelling leaves and actual spices, which you can use in sachets in your linen cupboard or clothes drawer, or put in a bowl or jar to scent the air in your room.

Collect the flowers just before they reach their full maturity on a dry sunny day. Choose flowers with a strong scent, like roses, carnations, honeysuckle, lavender, stocks and pinks. Collect the leaves of scented plants like rosemary, sweet bay, lemon verbena and geranium.

Pick the petals off the flower-heads and spread them out to dry in single layers on a sheet of paper. If you dry them outside, do not put them in the direct sunlight. Dry the leaves separately. Take the petals and leaves in at night or the dew will make them damp. The flowers should dry papery and keep most of their colour. The leaves will be crisper and you will need to remove them from their stalks and rub them through a sieve to make them ready for the pot-pourri.

Some pot-pourri recipes include the dried skin of oranges and lemons. You need to pare the skin very thinly and dry it in a very low oven on a baking tray. If your cooker has a warming drawer this is the best place. Chop the dried peel as finely as you can.

Mix the petal, ground leaves and peel together gently. Leave them for a day. Add pinches of allspice, ground cloves and $\frac{1}{2}$ teaspoon of orris root (which you can buy at a good chemist). The orris root helps to preserve the fragrance of the pot-pourri.

If you want to put your pot-pourri into sachets, break it down with a rolling pin. Make little bags in fine cloth, fill them and sew them up.

Use pot-pourri too in a pretty glass bowl or glass jar. Stir the contents occasionally to release the fragrance into the room.

Crystallized flowers

Gather bright fresh flowers, like violets, delphinium florets, or small rosebuds.

Boil together a measuring cupful of water and $\frac{1}{2}$ kg (1 lb) of sugar to make a syrup. Use a sugar thermometer, and when the syrup reaches 127°C (260°F) drop the flowers in a few at a time and boil for a minute. Turn off the heat. Lift the flowers out on a strainer spoon and lay them on greaseproof paper. Dry them off in a very cool oven or the warming drawer of the stove. Store them in a pretty box with sheets of greaseproof paper between each layer.

If you are wondering what they are for, the answer is – to eat. I expect you have seen hand-made chocolates with sugar flowers on top. This is how the very best ones are made.

Preserving flowers

In every country where summer gives way to winter and flowers wither and die, people try to keep flowers through into the winter months to decorate their homes.

Flowers and leaves unfortunately lose their colour when they are pressed and dried, so plan for a colour change to beige, brown and yellow tones and you won't be disappointed. You can also preserve grasses, seed-heads and, for a short time only, berries. Dried ears of corn and small fir-cones can often be mixed in with dried flowers and leaves.

There are a number of different ways of preserving plants which you may like to try.

Pressing

This is probably the best-known and safest method, especially with leaves. Pick the flowers or leaves as dry as possible (so this is not a rainy day activity!). Lay them between sheets of blotting paper or paper towels and place the sheets at intervals between the pages of a heavy book. Close the book and put a heavy weight, such as other books or bricks, on top of it. Leave it for three or four weeks without peeking in to see how the work is progressing. Your pressed flowers or leaves will then be ready to use.

When you have experimented a bit with different flowers and leaves, you may find with some that pulling off petals of the flower-head and pressing them, and then putting them back together later, is more satisfactory. You may also find that some of the bulkier flowers and leaves are difficult to preserve by this method.

Air-drying

For these bulkier plants and for grasses this is often a better preserving method. When you are going to air-dry plants you should cut them with long stems. Tie them tightly together in small bunches and hang them head downwards in a cool, dry, dark place.

Some of the plants which are best suited to this method and which you might like to encourage your family to grow are: white, yellow, pink and mauve statice; orange Chinese lanterns; honesty (work the dry seed pods off between finger and thumb to leave the

statice   Chinese lanterns   honesty

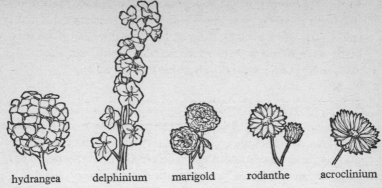

| hydrangea | delphinium | marigold | rodanthe | acroclinium |

'silver pennies'); pink and blue cornflowers; hydrangeas (which will lose most of their colour); young delphinium and larkspur heads; golden rod; and golden and orange marigolds. The best known 'everlasting' flowers grown for drying are rodanthe and acrolinium.

Drying in powder

Because you have to buy the materials for this method it is comparatively expensive, but you may like to make the investment to see the effect. The powder used is powdered borax or silica gel which you can buy in chemists. You will also need a box like a plastic freezer box or a biscuit tin.

Cover the bottom of the box with powder and lay the flowers face downwards in it. Pour powder over the flowers until they are completely embedded, and lift leaves and petals carefully to let the powder filter in underneath. Put the lid on the box and leave for three weeks if using borax, but only three days for silica gel. Take the dry, brittle flowers out with great care.

In the nineteenth century a similar method to this was developed in Erfurt in Germany, a centre of flower growing. Instead of borax they used fine, dry sand which had been washed clear of all impurities, dried by the fire or in an oven and sieved. The flowers are stood in a layer of sand in a tall box and the box is filled above the level of the flower-heads with sand. This is done with the aid of a funnel and a sieve so that the sand can be fed in right around the flowers without crumpling them. Store very carefully in a warm, dry place until the flowers are dry, which will take about two or three weeks. Tip the box so that the sand runs out and you can lift the flowers out by their stems. The flowers will be very brittle at first, but will absorb enough moisture from the atmosphere in a few days to become more flexible.

Preserving leaves with glycerine

For this method you need to buy the preserving material, but you only need a little glycerine and you can buy it quite cheaply at a chemist. The advantage of this method is that the leaves retain more colour and sheen.

When you bring your leaf sprays home, split the stems about 5 cm (2 in) up and stand the leaves in warm water for a few hours. Use only those leaves which have not begun to curl by then.

Now stand the sprays in a mixture of one part glycerine to two parts hot water so it is about 5–8 cm (2–3 in) deep. Use a jam jar, so that you won't need much of the solution. Stand the jar in a bucket or vase so that the weight of the branches won't drag the jar over. Let the leaves absorb the glycerine solution for about three weeks.

A Christmas nosegay

Here is a Victorian recipe for preserving flowers for Christmas and throughout the winter. You will need to make your preparations in mid-summer.

You need a wooden box with a lid which has no chinks or cracks. Make it as air-tight as possible. You may be able to find a biscuit tin or plastic freezer box large enough, or you could use a strong cardboard box which would survive storage in a dampish place, like an outhouse, cellar or unheated garage. Make sure that no light or air can get into the box.

Now line the box with paper (either newspaper or tissue paper). Put in a layer of fresh-cut flowers. Fill the box with alternate layers of paper and flowers. Put the lid on tightly and store the box in your chosen damp place. If all goes well, at Christmas 'you will have a nosegay as beautiful as in the middle of the summer', according to a writer in 1862.

Skeleton leaves

In China they have for many centuries painted the most beautiful skeleton leaves with delicate pictures. The process was probably introduced to Britain by way of Italy in the time of Queen Elizabeth I.

Skeleton leaves are exquisite and long lasting; the process of 'skeletonizing' is smelly and unattractive. The flesh of the leaves has to be rotted away to leave the basic structure which holds the whole leaf together. You can count yourself successful if you manage to come up with satisfactory specimens from half the leaves you start with.

One basic rule is not to mix the leaves from different trees together unless you know a lot about them. The leaves of the oak, chestnut, walnut and birch, for instance, contain so much tannin that they will actually act as a preservative on other leaves and stop their decomposition. You also want to start with the most perfect leaves in order to end up with good specimens.

You will need a number of containers as macerating vessels (to 'macerate' is to make soft by soaking), one for each type of leaf. Put your leaves in the containers and cover them with soft water or rain-water and leave them in a warm, sunny place. If you find that the leaves are floating up, lay a thick pad of doubled-up newspaper on them to keep them down in the water. Leave the containers undisturbed for six weeks. Make a note to yourself on a calendar or in your diary to remind you when to go back to them, and warn the family about what you are up to so that they don't empty the containers, thinking they are just full of messy water.

At the end of this period the containers will be full of an unpleasant mass of rotting and smelly vegetable matter. Pick out a few leaves with your hands if you can bear to, use a wooden spoon if you can't. Holding one leaf between thumb and finger, dip it into a bowl of warm, fresh water and rub the leaf to remove the rotting green matter and expose the leaf's skeleton. With the firmer leaves an old toothbrush will help you to clean off the skeleton.

Not all the leaves will come clean at the first washing. So put them back in your macerating vessel for another two or three weeks and then repeat the cleaning process. The second macerating session will be less noxious than the first, so don't be discouraged!

Leave the skeleton leaves in water until you can dry them out between paper towels. If you lay them down while they are wet, they will stick firmly where they lie. Some tough leaves will take longer than others. Ivy, on the other hand, surprisingly does not. Ivy leaves have a tough outer layer, filled with the usual green cells. The inner leaf will dissolve, leaving the outer skin like a bladder filled with green water. Tear this skin off gently to release the water and the skeleton will float out.

You may wish to bleach your leaves to make them whiter. Stand them stem down in a mild bleach solution for about four to six hours. You are recommended to use a glass jar for the bleaching so that you will be able to see how the process is going without touching the leaves. Rinse the leaves off in clean, warm water and then dry them again carefully. With delicate leaves it is wise to finish off the drying in the pages of a book or magazine so that they don't curl.

How to use preserved flowers and leaves

You will no doubt have all sorts of things that you want to do with your flowers or other plants. Here are a few further ideas.

1 Flowers, grasses, seed-heads and berries (which you should cover with a thin coat of lacquer or varnish just after picking) can be made into pretty, everlasting bouquets tied with ribbon to make beautiful and unusual presents. Add a lacey doiley for a 'Victorian bouquet'.

2 You can make table decorations and wreaths by fixing flower-heads, grasses and fir-cones tightly together in a wire frame.

3 Make bookmarks, calendars and pictures by mounting pressed flowers and leaves on cards. Use small amounts of a latex glue like Cow gum to fix the flowers in position. (To get rid of any unwanted patches of glue, make yourself a gum rubber by allowing a teaspoonful of glue to dry out, and rolling it into a ball. The gum rubber will pick up the unwanted glue for you.) Smooth a sheet of clear adhesive plastic very carefully over the card when the picture is complete. This will act as 'picture glass'.

4 Make greetings cards with pressed flowers, skeleton leaves, grasses etc.

5 Some people spray their skeleton leaves with gold or silver spray before mounting them.

6 A big bunch of dried leaves with grasses, honesty and Chinese lanterns makes a lovely room decoration. You can keep it all the year round or wrap the leaves very carefully in tissue paper and store them in a big cardboard box until you need them to replace the flowers of summer again.

Decorating eggs

Since pre-Christian times eggs have been a sign of spring and the rebirth of life in the land. That is why eggs have become associated with the Christian festival of Easter – the time when Jesus died and was reborn.

In many countries the giving of eggs as gifts has been part of the celebration of spring. Often these eggs are dyed or decorated. In Russia when spring began to take over from the long, long, dreary winter people went from house to house giving and receiving eggs and renewing acquaintances. It was in Russia that one of the world's most famous jewellers brought the decorated egg to its finest peak. Fabergé made intricate eggs of gold and silver set with precious jewels. Inside the beautiful 'shell' would be a tiny bejewelled picture.

But egg decorating was really a folk art of ordinary people who decorated ordinary eggs, and this is what we are telling you about here. You can use either hard-boiled or blown eggs.

Blowing eggs

Use eggs which have been kept at room temperature for at least a day. Hold your egg or put it in an egg cup. Pierce it with a needle or large pin at both ends. Make the hole at the large end slightly larger by working round it with the pin. If your pin is long enough use it to pierce the yolk of the egg. Shake the egg to mix the contents. Holding the egg very carefully over a bowl, blow through the smaller hole so that the contents come out at the other end.

Continue to blow into the egg until all the yolk and white has gone out through the larger hole. Rinse the inside of the egg under the tap. Stand it in an eggbox or egg cup so all the water can drain out. You can, of course, now make yourself a meal of scrambled eggs with the contents.

Hard-boiled eggs

A good way to boil eggs so that their shells won't crack is to put them in a pan of cold, salted water. Turn on the heat and boil for at least fifteen minutes, making sure that the pan doesn't boil dry. You can add a few drops of vegetable dye to the water if you want to colour the eggs as they boil. For egg decorating you will normally want to use white-shelled eggs.

Painted eggs

A very effective modern medium for painting blown eggs is the felt-tip pen. We suggest you use them at this stage, although you may want to try other paints later on.

Some people like to draw the design on to the egg-shell first with a pencil before colouring it in. Others like to paint directly on to the shell.

When you have painted the egg all over, and it has dried off, varnish it with clear nail varnish. This will keep the colours bright and shiny. To do this, hold the egg while standing it on the lower half. Upturn it and varnish it at the other end.

Czechoslovakian designs

In many countries the idea of the egg as a symbol of the start of life is combined with some sort of circle round the egg to express eternity and eternal life. Eggs in countries such as Czechoslovakia are often decorated with other symbols which represent religious themes and springtime.

You can make a circle round the egg with the help of a rubber band. Choose one which fits round the egg firmly but not too tightly. You don't want to break your carefully blown egg! Draw the circle on either side of the band with a pencil. Experiment with moving the band around to make other lines.

Some of the symbols which you will see on eggs are the fish, the symbol of Christ; the Sun, representing the idea of light coming to the earth;

flowers and leaves, to show the coming of spring;
and waves, which are another symbol for eternity.

Bejewelled eggs

Of course you may never be an artist like the great Fabergé, but
you could make your own 'bejewelled' eggs in simple materials.

Collect together tiny glass beads, sequins, tiny shells, even seeds.
You might also use little pieces of braid, lace, ribbon, tinsel, and
glitter dust. You will need a good adhesive too.

Use blown eggs. Paint them all over in one colour. You could use
felt-tip pen and clear nail varnish or you could use coloured nail
varnish alone. You can buy green, blue and silver varnish as well
as the more usual reds and pinks. You will find them quite
expensive but you might be able to collect some nearly finished
bottles from friends.

Trace out your pattern on the painted egg in pencil. Use a
toothpick or a cocktail stick to put little dots and thin lines of glue
where you want the 'jewels' to go. Pick the beads up by
dampening your finger, and place them in position.

If you want to hang your jewelled eggs up to display them to best
advantage, knot a thread, run it through a bead, up through one
egg, then put a few divider beads on to the thread and put another
egg above them. Leave enough thread at the top to form a loop for
hanging the eggs.

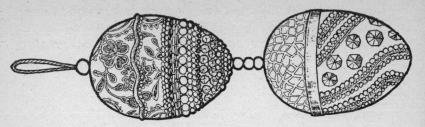

So far we have told you how to use blown eggs only. Here are ideas for decorating hard-boiled eggs. You may have wondered how long the eggs will keep if they still have the egg inside the shell. The answer is that if you have really cooked them hard the inside will gradually dry out and will not rot. But you must be sure to make them quite hard or one day someone may get a nasty surprise!

Patchwork eggs

As we have said, egg decorating is a folk art of central Europe and it was from there that the craft was taken to American when many German people settled in Pennsylvania. Both patchwork and scratch pattern eggs are made in America. For patchwork eggs you need tiny scraps of cotton cloth, a clean, firm glue and a damp cloth. You use hard-boiled eggs.

Spread the glue thinly over a small area and lay on a scrap. Press it down on to the shell with the damp cloth. Glue the next area and lay the next scrap, overlapping very slightly. Continue gluing, putting on scraps and pressing them down until you have covered the egg completely. Leave the egg so that the glue dries out. Then cover the egg with a thin layer of clear glue to make sure that all the edges really hold down flat.

Scratch pattern eggs

This is another German method of egg decorating.

Boil white eggs in a strong dye so that they are coloured as darkly as possible. Leave the eggs to cool. Pencil your design on the egg. Using a tool like a sharp nail or the pointed end of a nail file, scratch gently along the pencil lines so that you work through the layer of dye down to the white shell. Work several times along each line to get the effect that you want. Varnish the egg with clear nail varnish. Traditionally the designs for these eggs included the name of the person to whom they were to be given and the date of the year in which the egg was decorated. Nowadays such an egg could make a very unusual birthday greeting.

Dyed decorations

For these eggs you cover parts of the shell before you boil them in the dye so that the shape covered does not 'take' the dye.

For flower-patterned eggs you will need to collect together some small leaves and flowers and you will need a pair of old nylon tights or stockings cut into lengths.

Dip the uncooked egg in cooking oil, taking care not to knock it. Press the flowers against the shell of the egg and while holding them in position put the egg in a length of nylon stocking so that it and the oil holds the plant against the shell. Tie both ends of the stocking tightly with thread to make a tight little parcel. You may need an extra pair of hands to help! You can also use pieces of cloth to block out the dye from the shell.

Put the eggs into a cold water dye. Bring the water to the boil and boil for at least fifteen minutes. The longer you boil the egg, the stronger the dye will become.

Remove the egg parcels from the dye and put them into cold water. When they are cool remove the stocking wrapper. The shape of the flower or leaves will show white or much lighter than the rest of the egg. Varnish the egg with clear nail varnish.

Thread decorated eggs

This sort of egg decoration originated in Russia. For this you need some old material which you know is not fast-dyed. I think that this sort of material may have been more common in the old days than it is now.

Unravel the material so you can use the threads. Collect as many colours as you wish, but you can use just one colour. Wind the thread round your egg so that it criss-crosses down the egg. Wrap a piece of cloth round the whole egg and cook it for fifteen minutes in boiling water.

The pattern of the thread network will come out on the egg. This is fun to do but perhaps not as pretty as some of the others, so you might like to have this egg to eat!

Displaying eggs

Once you have become skilful in making decorated eggs, you may like to use them together to make other decorations and to display them.

You can string the blown eggs on a thread which you pass on a long needle through the blow-holes. You can separate the eggs from each other with beads or pieces of painted macaroni.

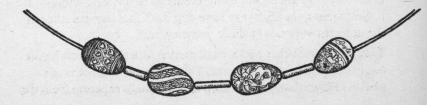

You can use them to make mobiles in the same way as some people use ping-pong balls, or you can hang them from the twigs of a white-painted branch to make an Easter tree or even a rather unusual Christmas tree. Alternatively you can use them on a Christmas tree as hanging decorations.

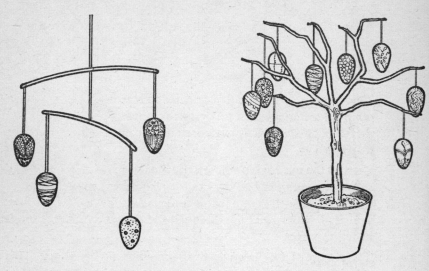

Shellcraft

Shells are often very beautiful in themselves, so it is a pleasure to collect them even if you never get round to using them! But if you do use them, there are all sorts of things that you can make.

Collecting shells

If you don't live near the sea and can't get to it easily, it is possible to buy shells from some craft shops. If you can collect them yourself, time your visit so that you know the tide is going out, or your treasure will be hidden by the water. Follow the water down as it reveals the shells and the depressions in the sand which indicate that a shellfish may have dug itself in. Here are some of the different varieties of shells you may find.

Take a plastic bucket and a small garden fork or spade with you to dig the shells out of the sand. Take an assortment of small plastic bags so that you can keep delicate shells separate from the

GASTROPODS

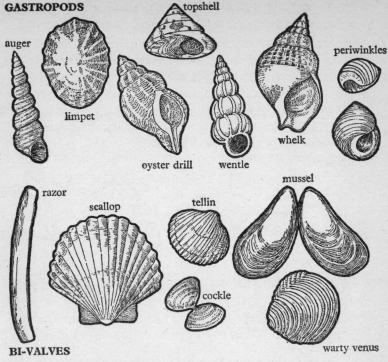

auger

topshell

periwinkles

limpet

oyster drill

wentle

whelk

razor

scallop

tellin

mussel

cockle

BI-VALVES

warty venus

larger, heavier ones. A plastic colander or sieve is useful for washing the sand out of the shells in the water. As you gather your shells you will want to store those you are not using straight away. Collect boxes of various sizes, yoghurt cups and jars, and a bigger box to hold the smaller ones neatly. Put the shells of one size and kind together so you can find them easily while you are working with them. It's a good idea to label each container.

Shell jewellery

Making shell jewellery is really easy. For jewellery-making most people use gastropods, as the edges of the bi-valves tend to chip more easily.

You can buy ring, earring, key-ring and brooch bases at most craft shops. You can also buy chains, link rings and fasteners. At the same shop you will be able to buy a hard-setting adhesive to fix the shells to the bases. Follow the instructions on the glue carefully.

Now all you need to do is to glue the chosen shell or shells on to the base. But here comes the artistry. There are good and bad positions for each shell. If you are making a ring, put the ring base on your finger and move the shell round until it looks right to you, and will not spike or rub your other fingers. With earrings and key-rings make the same adjustments, making sure that both earrings in a pair look as much alike as you can possibly make them. For brooches you can get larger bases and can use a number of mixed small shells to make up a design.

When you are on the beach collecting shells, bring back a bag of sand. Keep it in a box or bowl and use it, dampened, to stand your jewellery in while the glue is drying. If you lay it down on the table, the shells will shift about before the glue is dry enough to hold them fast.

Shell bracelets and necklaces are rather more difficult to make, although you can buy bracelets made of linked-up bases, like this:

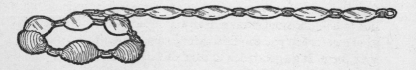

The problem with necklaces is that you have to make a hole in the shells in order to thread them together. Even if you are very careful, you are going to break some of your shells. You will need a darning needle or a pair of dividers, a small hammer and a wooden working surface. (Don't work on the formica kitchen tops or on a bare table or you will be very unpopular!) Working with the opening of the shell upwards, hold the sharp point of the needle on to the shell and tap gently with the hammer until the point pierces the shell.

Thread the shells on a strongish nylon thread long enough to go over your head, or make a shorter necklace which opens and closes with a ring clasp which you can buy in a craft shop.

You can also make a pendant necklace with one particularly fine shell hanging from a chain. If the shell is thick, you may need to ask someone who has a very fine drill to make the hole for you. You can buy links which will join the shell to the main chain so that it falls down flat. If you are using a bi-valve, you can either use just one half or you can glue the two halves back together with your adhesive.

Bracelets can be made in the same way as necklaces, although you will need an elasticated thread to allow you to pass the bracelet over your hand. You can also make 'charm' bracelets with a variety of small shells dangling from a bracelet chain at intervals on links.

Shell decorating

The most beautiful shell decorations are often the simplest. We have a huge pinky-cream gastropod that our son fished up off the coast of Mexico, which stands alone and perfect on the mantelpiece. Our feeling is that shells should on the whole be used in ways which show them as shells, but some people like to fix them together to make mice and funny people.

One summer our children decorated the tops of jam jars with shells stuck in a Polyfilla base. At Christmas they filled the jars with bath salts and gave them as presents. They would also look very nice filled with pebbles or shells and water.

You can also decorate the tops of the little, light wooden boxes that you can buy in craft shops. Don't try to decorate the sides, as the shells won't stay on for long if the box is used at all. Use the same sort of adhesive as you would use for jewellery-making. Lay the shells out on a sheet of paper in the design you want for your box top. Pick them up one at a time with a pair of tweezers and position them on the box. You might use a few beach pebbles with the shells.

Shell pictures

There are two sorts of picture you can make with shells. One sort is really a way of displaying your shell collection, the other uses the shells to create pictures or designs.

You will need a backing board the same size as the paper you would use for painting a picture. This can be strong card, hardboard or a sheet of plywood. It can be left plain, it can be varnished or painted, or it can be covered with cloth. Choose to suit your own project.

If you want to make a display picture you will need a variety of shells with different shapes, sizes and colours. Plan the layout on a sheet of paper the same size as your backing board. Leave a good margin all round – you don't want the shells to be crowding out along the edges. If you plan to frame your picture, you will need to leave an even wider margin. Fix the shells into position on the

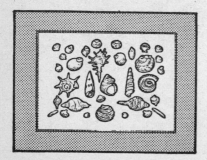

picture board and leave them so that the glue can dry firmly. Use a strong adhesive which is not too runny when it comes out of the tube or tin.

You may like to write out a 'key' which indicates what the shells are and possibly where and when you collected them. You can make other pictures in the same way, using the shells to build up flowers, animals, scenes or more formal designs. You can add other related material to your pictures, such as pebbles, bits of dried seaweed, string, even areas of sand sprinkled on to the adhesive.

Natural dyes

The art of dyeing yarns and cloths is so ancient that no one could claim that their country was the home of the craft. Indian squaws were certainly expert in the use of plants, seeds, roots and nuts as dyes, and passed on their skills to the American women who spun their own wool and then dyed it with homemade colours.

It will probably take you much longer to dye something using vegetable dyes than it would if you used a shop-bought dye. However, it is worth the effort as the results are natural, rich, glowing colours – dandelion yellow, geranium pink, fern green, elderberry blue. You will have the satisfaction of having made the colours yourself, and they even smell nice!

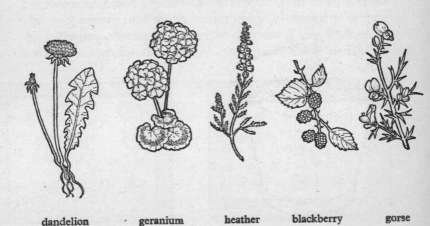

dandelion   geranium   heather   blackberry   gorse

You can collect suitable material for dyeing all year round, but the best time is the beginning of summer when you can gather young, healthy plants, leaves, flower-heads, roots, stalks and barks. Bracken, gorse and heather will give you various shades of yellow; geranium head, a pale pink; birch leaves, a greenish yellow; blackberries, a blue shade, and you can get a purple from dandelion roots. There are many other plants you can use but different plants need to be treated in slightly different ways before they will give up their beautiful colours. You should aim to collect at least $\frac{1}{2}$ kg (1 lb) of your chosen dye material as this will dye $\frac{1}{2}$ kg (1 lb) of dry wool.

Preparing the wool

The preparation of the material to be dyed is very important as you want the result to be 'fast', which means that it won't lose its colour in the wash and dye other clothes! It is better to start your experiments with wool, which is easier to prepare than silk or cotton and you are more likely to get an even effect. The wool must first be 'scoured' to get rid of any dirt or grease, which means washing the wool in a warm soapy mixture and rinsing it well. You will find the wool easier to manage if you tie it in loose figure-of-eight skeins.

Mordanting

The wool needs another important treatment before it is able to absorb the dye, and this is known as mordanting. There are several different mordants, but the one most often used is alum (potassium aluminium sulphate) – you should be able to get this at a chemist. For $\frac{1}{2}$ kg (1 lb) of wool, dissolve thoroughly 100 g (4 oz) of alum and 25 g (1 oz) cream of tartar in a large pan of water (make sure the two are well mixed). Put the pan on a hot-plate of the stove and when the water is warm put the wool in. It doesn't matter if it is still wet after the scouring process! Bring the water slowly to the boil, and let it simmer for one hour. Don't be tempted to stir it too much, once or twice is enough. But keep an eye on it to make sure it doesn't boil dry. Use a stick to lift the wool from the pan and gently squeeze out the excess water. The mordanting is now finished and you can either dye the wool straight away or leave it overnight in a cloth or plastic bag to keep it damp.

Dyeing

The next step is preparing your chosen dye. Berries need to be crushed and stems, roots, leaves and twigs have to be chopped into small pieces. Put your chosen plant material into a large pan of cold water, bring it to the boil (some plants need to be steeped in the cold water before heating), and simmer for about one or two hours. The length of simmering time again depends on the plant you are using. The yellow colours generally need less time, whilst bark, twigs and roots take longer and should be soaked in cold water for twelve hours before boiling.

Put your wool in the dye bath using two clean, smooth sticks. Don't stir the wool around but leave it to absorb as much dye as possible. It is best to leave the wool in the pan until the dye is quite cold. Lift the wool out using the two sticks again – rubber gloves would also be a help – and gently squeeze out the excess dye. Rinse the wool thoroughly until the water is perfectly clear, and then leave it to dry.

There are lots of different things you can use your wool for, such as knitting, crocheting and weaving. Why don't you use it to make the crochet tabard on page 58?

Making decorations

People have been able to buy Christmas decorations made from glass, paper and other materials for many years, but making your own decorations is much more fun than buying them. Some will last from year to year if you wrap them carefully in tissue paper and store them in boxes. Others will last only for a season until they grow dry and dusty. Here are a few ideas for traditional decorations made with natural materials.

A calenigg

Christmas balls made of leaves and cones, called caleniggs, used to be carried round by children on Christmas Eve to greet the neighbours and wish them good cheer. In return, as with carol singing, money was given to the children for the poor. You can use caleniggs nowadays as table decorations.

You need a grapefruit or large orange for the base, four straight sticks sharpened at one end for the stand and handle by which the calenigg is carried, ears of corn, holly, evergreen twigs and cones for decoration, and a candle.

Push the sticks into the fruit. Make holes in the fruit with a knitting needle or skewer for the corn stalks, holly and evergreen twigs. Add cones which are still on a short stem. Cut out a hole in the top so you can stand the candle steady. If you have dried some everlasting flowers, you could add these to the decoration. You can add tinsel and small silver or gold balls if you wish.

Crystal covered leaves

At Christmas we decorate the house with evergreens – over pictures, in vases, on shelves. Nowadays there are spray-on canisters of gold, silver and white paint with which you can decorate the evergreens. The Victorians had no such things. Their recipe for making the evergreens glitter was as follows.

Make up light sprays of evergreen and suspend them by a network of strings so they hang into but do not touch the sides of a deep bucket. Put a pound of alum (which you can buy at the chemist) into the bucket. Pour a gallon of boiling water over it and leave the bucket over night.

In the morning remove the sprays. You will need to be very careful or you will knock off the crystals which have formed. A Victorian writer once described the sprays and garlands as 'glittering with minute crystals resembling diamonds'.

Victorian tree decorations

The Victorians often made their own Christmas tree ornaments such as gilded nuts and little nests.

Gilded nuts. In the nineteenth century they gilded walnuts by painting them all over with white of egg, using a feather as a brush, and then rolling the nuts in leaf gold 'until well covered'.

Here is a modern version for you to try. First hammer a long, thin nail or tack into one end of the nut, from which you can later tie a ribbon. Then cover the nut with a very thin layer of glue which will later dry transparent. Roll the nut in glitter and suspend it from the tree with a very narrow red or purple ribbon.

Birds' nests. In a book published in 1867 the instructions for making a bird's nest start, 'Get the cook to give you some halves of unboiled egg-shells', and go on to use 'handfuls of moss'. Over a century later we say take some half egg-shells when your family are having scrambled eggs, and suggest that if moss is not readily available, you take some dark green crêpe paper and cut it up into tiny pieces to use as a substitute. In the Victorian instructions you dip the shell in egg white (we suggest glue), make a hollow of moss in your hand (hold the crêpe paper shavings in your hand) and put the half shell in it. The moss (crêpe paper shavings) will adhere to the outside very well. Line the egg inside with feathers (or cotton wool) and when dry, you can fill the 'nest' with sugar eggs.

As the Victorian writer said, 'These nests look charming in the foliage of a Christmas tree; tiny hands delightedly grasp them, and, alas! soon succeed in discovering of what they are made.'

Fruit pyramid

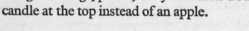

In Spain pyramids of oranges, interspersed with shiny green leaves are made in pottery as well as with fresh fruit. In America pyramids of green or red apples decorate Christmas tables. Fruit is not cheap and if left too long will spoil, so build your table pyramid for a special occasion and eat the fruit soon after. You can make a special stand for the fruit pyramid. You will almost certainly need some help with this unless you are used to using a drill. You need a 30-cm (12-in) log of wood, which has been carefully sawn so that it stands straight and steady, and several wooden skewers, pointed at both ends, some longer than others.

Drill holes at intervals straight through the log and push the skewers through, the longer ones nearer the bottom. Put half a skewer into the top of the log.

Fix the apples, starting at the bottom, on to the skewers through the stem ends and fix one apple on the top. Fill the gaps with evergreen twigs, privet, holly or laurel. You could perhaps use a candle at the top instead of an apple.

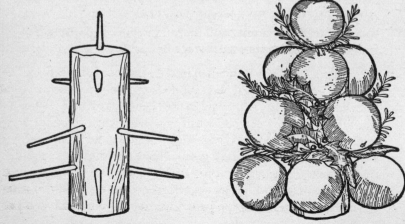

Popcorn chains

An American traditional decoration is popcorn chains. You can buy tins of corn to pop yourself according to the instructions on the tin (which is great fun), or you can buy packets of plain or honeyed popcorn. You need a long darning needle threaded with strong white cotton and, if you want to make a number of chains, some assistance. Put all the popped corn in a big bowl and sit round it threading most of it on to your needles. We say 'most' of it because you will obviously need to eat some of it too! One of the added pleasures of this sort of chain is that when the sad moment comes when the decorations must be taken down, you can eat them (if they haven't become soggy or dusty in the festive atmosphere!).

A kissing bough

A sprig of mistletoe traditionally gives people the right to kiss anybody who is standing under it. By custom, when a young man kissed a girl under the mistletoe, he picked off one of the white berries from the sprig and when there were no more berries left, there was no more kissing.

The kissing bough is a sort of cross between the mistletoe sprig and the Christmas tree, which it pre-dates as a Christmas decoration. Originally kissing boughs were built up on a framework of reeds or straw and carried candles. Nowadays you will find wire easier to work with, and you may decide that dripping candle-wax and the dangers of fire make candles unsuitable.

You can make the frame by unbending a couple of wire coathangers, cutting them into suitable lengths with clippers and fixing them into circles. Bind the wire together to hold the circles. Tie the circles together within each other to make the round base shape.

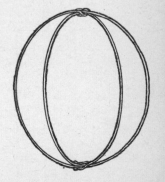

Collect sprays from evergreen trees, holly, laurel, mistletoe, some small fir-cones, some silver Christmas tree balls and a metre or so of bright satin ribbon. Tie the ribbon as a loop and bow at the top of the frame. Tie the sprigs of evergreen on to the framework, packing them together as tightly as possible. Tie the silver balls and fir-cones in among the greenery. Hang the sprig of mistletoe at the bottom of the bough.

Hang your bough from the looped ribbon in a suitable place where the taller members of the family won't bump into it.

Where to buy your supplies

We give you here the names and addresses of a number of craft shops scattered throughout the country. There are of course many more. Some of these shops run a mail order service, so that if you are not near a craft supplier you can write off for a catalogue to the shop you think most likely to supply your needs and get them to send what you want by post. But catalogues cost money. So you will have to write first and ask them how much they charge for the catalogue, which will depend on how simple or luxurious it is.

Most of these shops are general craft suppliers. A few of them are specialist shops which we have included because they supply crafts which not all shops cater for, or because they have a particularly wide range of good materials for a particular craft.

At the start you may well not need to go to a specialist craft supplier for your chosen craft, as the materials you need may be readily available in ordinary shops, but as you progress you will probably want to use more professional materials.

Aberdeen

The Craft Centre, 97 Claremont Street, Aberdeen, Scotland
Open daily 9.30–5.30 and from 9 on Saturdays.
Catalogue and mail order.
Materials for beadwork, candlemaking, leatherwork, batik, macramé, tapestry, embroidery, jewellery-making, and a wide range of craft books.

Birmingham

See page 142 for the many branches of
The Midland Educational Co Ltd

Burnley

Northern Handicrafts Ltd, Belle Vue Mill, Westgate, Burnley, Lancashire
Open 9–5.30 Monday to Thursday, 9–4.30 Friday.
Catalogue and mail order.
Embroidery and needlework materials and accessories, materials for leatherwork, jewellery-making, beadwork and egg decórating.

Canterbury

The Handicraft Shop, 83 Northgate, Canterbury, Kent
Open daily 9–5.30 with a half day on Thursday.
Supplies for needlework, tapestry, crochet, macramé, leatherwork, candlemaking and jewellery work.

Dorchester

Frank Herring and Sons, 27 High Street, Dorchester, Dorset
Open Monday to Saturday 9–5.30 but closed all day on Thursday.
Catalogue and mail order.
They specialize in materials and equipment for spinners and weavers.

Glasgow

Miller's (Arts and Crafts) Ltd, 54 Queen Street, Glasgow, Scotland
Open daily 9–5.30.
No catalogue but they will accept orders by post.
Materials for leatherwork, needlework and tapestry, crochet, macramé, tie-dye and batik.

Harrogate

Arts and Handicrafts, 18 Station Parade, Harrogate, North Yorkshire
Open daily 9–5.30 with early closing on Wednesday.
Materials for jewellery work, beadwork, brass rubbing, macramé, shellcraft, candlemaking, pottery and paper crafts.

Huddersfield

Arts and Crafts, 10–11 Byram Street, Huddersfield, West Yorkshire
Open daily 9–5.30 with a half day on Wednesday.
Catalogue and mail order.
Materials for macramé, beadwork, needlework, candlemaking, and jewellery-making.

Hull

Handicrafts of Hull, 20 Hepworth Arcade, Silver Street, Hull, Humber
Open 9–5 daily.
Materials for leatherwork, needlework, jewellery-making, crochet, tie-dye and candlemaking.

Lancaster

Leisure Crafts, 14 Church Street, Lancaster, Lancashire
Open daily 9.30–5.30 with a half day on Wednesday.
Materials for leatherwork, tapestry, candlemaking, batik and paper crafts.

London

Crafts Unlimited, 178 Kensington High Street, London w8
Open 9–5.30 Monday to Friday and 9–5 Saturday.
Catalogue and mail order. (Their mail order service is from Dryad Ltd, PO Box 38, Northgates, Leicester.)
Tools and materials for jewellery-making, paperwork, leatherwork, pottery, weaving, macramé, candlemaking, patchwork, embroidery and needlework. Craft books and a large number of pamphlets on a variety of crafts.

The Fulham Pottery, 210 King's Road, sw6
Open Monday to Friday 9–1 and 2–4.45 and 9–11.45 on Saturdays.
Catalogue and mail order.
This pottery has been active for three centuries! They have all the materials a potter requires and will also give advice to callers.

The Handweavers Studio and Gallery Ltd, 29 Haroldstone Road, London e17
Open Tuesday to Saturday 10–5 and until 9 on Saturdays.
The studio stocks materials and equipment for the weaver, and runs

weekend and summer courses to teach weaving and tapestry. They also give lectures and demonstrations to parties from schools.

Hobby Horse Ltd, 15–17 Langton Street, London SW10
Open 10–5.30 daily.
Catalogue and mail order.
Materials for beadwork, jewellery-making, leatherwork, macramé, candlemaking, batik and other crafts. Books on crafts.

Homecraft Supplies Ltd, 27 Trinity Road, London SW17
Open 8.30–4.30 Monday to Friday.
Catalogue and mail order.
Materials and tools for leatherwork, embroidery, crochet and needlework.

The Needlewoman Shop, 146–8 Regent Street, London W1
Open 9–5.30 daily and until 7 on Thursday.
Catalogue and mail order.
Materials, tools and kits for all forms of needlework, and for crochet, patchwork and beadwork. Craft books, pamphlets and patterns.

Phillips and Page Ltd, 50 Kensington High Street, London W8
For mail order: 40 Elm Hill, Norwich, Norfolk
This is 'the' brass rubbing shop with all the necessary materials and lots of books about the craft. Helpful advice readily available. They have a large number of pamphlets produced by Studio 69 which give comprehensive details of figure brasses county by county. The guides tell you where the brasses are, who will give permission for rubbing and what fees are charged.

The Pot Shop, 8 Shillingford Street, London N1
Open daily 10–6 with a half day on Thursday.
Pottery materials but also materials for brass rubbing, candlemaking and some other crafts and a very interesting selection of materials for doll making.

Manchester

The Handicraft Centre, 37 Lever Street, Manchester
Open 9–5 Monday to Friday and 9–4 on Saturday.
Catalogue and mail order.
Materials for embroidery, tapestry, beadwork, macramé, batik, candlemaking, leatherwork and jewellery-making. Craft books and pamphlets.

Nelson

J. W. Coates and Co Ltd, Albert Street, Warehouse, Nelson, Lancashire
This is a mail order company that will send you their catalogue of remnant parcels suitable for patchwork, appliqué and collage work, embroidery, tie-dye and batik. If you live locally, you can arrange to pick up your parcel to save the postage.

Norwich

Phillips and Page Ltd, 40 Elm Hill, Norwich, Norfolk
See pages 79 and 139.

Nottingham

King's Handicrafts, 122 Chilwell Road, Beeston, Nottingham
Open daily 9.30–5.30, closed for lunch 12.45–1.30. Closed all day Monday.
Materials for crochet, tapestry, macramé, leatherwork, needlework, and candlemaking.

Reading

Reading Fine Art Gallery, 81 London Street, Reading, Berkshire
Open Monday to Friday 9–1 and 2.15–5.30. Closed Wednesday and Saturday at 1 pm.
Catalogue and mail order.
Materials for fabric printing, pottery, paper crafts, and drawing and painting materials.

Southampton

Hampshire Hobbies and Handicrafts, 46b Nichols Road, Six Dials, Southampton, Hampshire
Open Monday and Tuesday 10–5.30, Thursday–Saturday 9.30–5.30, closed Wednesday.
Materials for batik, beadwork, brass rubbing, jewellery work, pottery, leather work, macramé, shellwork, tapestry, tie-dye, weaving and paper crafts.

Stroud

Cotswold Craft Centre, Stroud, Gloucestershire
A mail order business only, with catalogue.
Materials for beadwork, shellcraft, jewellery-making, embroidery,
macramé, needlwork, tapestry and leatherwork. Occasional 'lucky dip'
parcels suitable for collage work.

Truro

The Hobby House, 2 Little Castle Street, Truro, Cornwall
Open 9–5 daily with a half day on Thursday.
No catalogue, but they will send you a duplicated list of their stock.
Mail order.
Materials for embroidery, tapestry, and macramé, and templates for
patchwork.

Watford

Allcraft, 11 Market Street, Watford, Hertfordshire
Open 9–5.30 daily.
Catalogue and mail order.
Materials for batik, tie-dye, beadwork, candlemaking and
jewellery-making. A choice of craft books.

Woking

Brewster and Co (Woking) Ltd, Arthur's Bridge Wharf, Woking,
Surrey
Open daily 8–5 with an extra hour on Friday and Saturday evenings.
Materials for beadwork, jewellery-making, brass rubbing, macramé,
candlemaking and shellcraft.

The Midland Educational Co Ltd is a large craft supplier with a number of branches throughout the country. They are all open 9–5.30 daily and until 6.30 on Thursday and 6 on Saturday. Mail orders accepted.
Materials for needlework, brass rubbing, tie-dye, batik, leather and leather-working tools and modelling clays.

The Midland Educational Co Ltd,
104 Corporation Street,
Birmingham, B4 6SZ

The Midland Educational Co Ltd,
71–73 Fairfax Street,
Bristol, BS1 3BQ

The Midland Educational Co Ltd,
10–11 High Street,
Stratford-upon-Avon,
Warwickshire

The Midland Educational Co Ltd,
1–5 City Arcade,
Coventry,
West Midlands

The Midland Educational Co Ltd,
152 The Parade,
Gracechurch Centre,
Sutton Coldfield,
West Midlands

Ratcliffe's Toyeries,
48 Queen's Street,
Derby

J. C. Bond,
26 High Street,
Kettering,
Northamptonshire

The Midland Educational Co Ltd,
17–19 Market Street,
Leicester, LE1 6DF

Mawson, Swan & Morgan,
Gray Street,
Newcastle-upon-Tyne,
Tyne & Wear

W. Mark Ltd,
27 The Drapery,
Northampton, NN1 2HA

Wildings,
33 Castle Street,
Shrewsbury, SY1 2BL,
Shropshire

The Midland Educational Co Ltd,
24–26 Station Road,
Solihull, B91 3SF,
West Midlands

More books to read

Using needle and thread

The Creative Art of Embroidery by Barbara Snook (Hamlyn)
Bargello by Geraldine Cosentino (Pan)
Zigzag Stitchery (Golden Hands)
Victorian Fancywork by Markrich and Kiewe (Pitman)
Beginning Patchwork by Dorothy Wright (Dryad Press)
Ideas for Patchwork by Suzy Ives (Batsford)
Beadwork From North American Indian Designs by M. Murphy
(Batsford)
Bead Threading and Bead Looming by Dixon and Ward (Search Press)
How To Do Beadwork by Mary White (Dover Publications)

Using colour and cloth

Appliqué by Evangeline Shears and Diantha Fielding (Pan)
Collage (Golden Hands)
Collage (Leisure Crafts Series, Search Press)
Batik: Art and Craft by Nik Krevitsky (Van Nostrand Reinhold)
Batik (Leisure Crafts Series, Search Press)
Rugmaking by Nell Znamierowski (Pan)
McCall's Book of Handicrafts by Nanina Comstock (Hamlyn)
Complete Book of Home Crafts edited by P. Westland (Ward Lock)

Using wool and string

Macramé by Mary Walker Phillips (Pan)
Introducing Macramé by E. Short (Batsford)
Macramé 1 and 2 (Leisure Crafts Series, Search Press)
Crochet by Emily Wildman (Pan)
Weaving by Nell Znamierowski (Pan)
Weaver's Craft by L. E. Simpson and M. Weir (Dryad Press)
Backstrap Weaving by B. Taber and M. Anderson (Pitman)

Using paper and paint

Pattern Making with Cut Paper by R. Grimshaw (Dryad Press)
The Paper Book by D. Munson and A. Ross (Kaye & Ward)
Chinese Kites by David Jue (Tuttle, Tokyo)
Kite Craft by L. and J. Newman (Allen & Unwin)
Brasses by Malcolm Cook (Shire Publications)
Brasses and Brass Rubbing by Clare Gittings (Blandford Press)
Brass Rubbing by Malcolm Norris (Pan)
Notes on Brass Rubbing edited by Catling (Ashmolean Museum, Oxford)

Using all sorts of materials

Imaginative Leatherwork by Jeanne Argent (David & Charles)
Leatherwork by I. P. Roseaman (Dryad Press)
Working with Leather (Leisure Crafts Series, Search Press)
Pottery by Jolyon Hofsted (Pan)
Pottery Without a Wheel by Keith Tyler (Dryad Press)
Candlemaking by Mary Carey (Pan)
The Candlemaker's Primer by K. Lomneth Chisholm (Robert Hale)
Introducing Candlemaking by Paul Collins (Batsford)
The Handicrafts of the Sailor by Steven Banks (David & Charles)
Make Things Sailor's Made by Marjorie Stapleton (Studio Vista)
Ships in Bottles by Donald Hubbard (David & Charles)

Using nature's harvest

Art of Dried and Pressed Flowers by P. Westland (Ward Lock)
Decorations from Dried Flowers and Grasses
(Leisure Crafts Series, Search Press)
Decorating Eggs (Leisure Crafts Series, Search Press)
Egg Craft by Arden J. Newsome (World's Work)
The Art of Shellcraft by Paula Critchley (Ward Lock)
Fun with Shells (Leisure Crafts Series, Search Press)
The Use of Vegetable Dyes by V. Thurston (Dryad Press)